Durham E-Theses

Birthing pains: How cyborgs refigure medical bodies, technologies, and objectives

Theoharis, Sotiria

How to cite:

Use policy

Academic Support Office, Durham University, University Office, Old Elvet, Durham DH1 3HP
e-mail: e-theses.admin@dur.ac.uk Tel: +44 0191 334 6107
http://etheses.dur.ac.uk

BIRTHING PAINS: HOW CYBORGS REFIGURE MEDICAL BODIES, TECHNOLOGIES, AND OBJECTIVES.

*...the aphrodisia are situated within the ancient thematic of
the relations between death, immortality, and reproduction.
(Foucault, 1988)*

SOTIRIA THEOHARIS
MASTER'S THESIS
DURHAM UNIVERSITY
SOCIOLOGY DEPT., 1997

Abstract: *Cyborgs are polymorphic and not yet visibly different from humans in part because cyborgic technologies have just been developed, in part because we are not trained to see how the post human arises. The birth of cyborgs alters the core of medicine from disease-containment and death-assessment to enhancement of function and image, to transgression of previous natural bounds as established by the possibility of space and oceanic travel. Cyborgs, as postmodern/ posthuman products of medicine, make visible the current shift in the construction of medical bodies, technologies, and objectives. Medical bodies have been determined by a conception of patienthood or diseased body. The connection of body and disease as distinct species happened in the medical enclosure: the hospital-clinic, during mid-late 19th century. In the hospital-clinic, the medical body has been clearly mapped in terms of disease identity or malfunction, and it has encountered medical technologies used to aid in diagnosis. The patient-doctor relationship has shifted because of the revolution in instrumentation at the turn of the century. Another shift can be discerned, as it is again mirrored in the relations of doctor-patient, as it has been re-structured through cyberspace and expert systems. Clearly, the revolution or scientification of medicine has been fueled by the tuberculosis crisis as it challenged medical and political institutions. A similar crisis has occurred with AIDS: is cyborg-technology the fulfillment of the modern dream of immortality and total control in the face of the epidemic? An easy answer to such question cannot be produced. Cyborgs are a product of the meeting of natural and human sciences through cybernetics. Their existence and proliferation destabilize assumptions at the philosophical foundations of knowledge and medicine as well as our conceptions of identity and rights, through an unsettling of the connection between community-individuality, of the distinction between private and public domains.*

Key words: *Cyborgs, Cybernetics, Medical Technologies, Expert Systems, Internet, Cyberspace, Patient-Doctor Relation, AIDS, Tuberculosis, Philosophy and History Of Medicine, Postmodern Theory, Sociology Of Knowledge/ Medicine, Feminism.*

Acknowledgements:

This project, foremost, would not be possible without the support of my family both emotionally and physically throughout a period of trial and academic uncertainty, and my former academic advisor Steve Fuller at Durham University, who has helped me clarify some of the very convoluted and at times too dense material. He has sharpened my arguments and usefully, poignantly criticized my thesis, both editorially and in terms of context. Useful commentary was provided by Roy Boyne as well, whom I had the opportunity to work with the last year of my attendance at Durham University. Finally, it is important to note the support and belief of many teachers and scholars along my path. People who have believed in my abilities: Carol Abate, Carla Freccero, Margo Hendricks, John Jordan, and last but not least Karen Wallace. Finally this project is intellectually indebted to Donna Haraway, whom I have recently met and with whom I am working, Michel Foucault, whom I did not have the opportunity to meet other than through his texts, and Adele Clarke, whom I have the pleasure of working with as I continue my Doctoral work at the University of California, San Francisco.

Contents

Preface / Introduction

Cyborg is the concept at the center of my work. Thus, it is important to understand how such concept is delimited, and how it should remain open not because of an inability to define it further, but rather because the forms through which cyborgs appear may differ in the future with inventions of technology. The argument that the most skeptical reader would put forth is that cyborgs are solely the product of science fiction and have nothing to do with medicine, its future, present, or past. I will suggest that cyborgs mark a more intimate interaction of artifact and organism (technology and medicine) to the point where the distinction of artifact/ organism becomes blurred, where one can only meaningfully talk about the techno-organic system, where the ontological separation of the two is pointless. In this regard, cyborgs are born by medical technologies when it is confronted with demands to transgress prior bounds such as death, a debilitating condition, or even to envision enhancements of human limitations with regard to space/ oceanic travel, with regard to perception, memory. I map the recent history of medicine in crisis to show that major technological innovations in the medical field occurred during times of social uncertainty (during epidemics) the main examples being *Tuberculosis* at the turn of the century and presently *AIDS*. Would the current products of medicine "in crisis" be termed cyborgic: terminally ill patients hooked up to life sustaining machines; a brain dead patient giving birth; bodies frozen in liquid nitrogen waiting their moment of rebirth; AIDS patients that need to constantly monitor their immune system (T-cell counts)?

Current medical products, beyond patients on the edge of death, include individuals with artificial limbs that enhance function or ones that have undergone cosmetic surgery to enhance image (artificial breasts, facial structures and so on) that demonstrate an enhanced commercial demand for prosthetic technologies. It is clear that one does not become cyborgic through necessity only but through the choice of enhancement as well. When I am talking about cyborgs, I am referring to an assemblage in which each element differs from the other in terms of degree and kind. From this diversity, however, one should not be inhibited to examine each individual as being cyborgic in its own right. Cyborgs differ from each other with regard to degree, i.e., how intimate is the connection between organic and technological: functional (artificial limbs), enhancing (breast implants), regulatory (pace maker), configuring (gene therapy),[1] and kind depending at the types of technologies involved, for example cyborgs resulting from any combination of such expertise: genetic engineering, cosmetic surgery, visionics, and so on.

---

[1] An adaptation of restorative, normalizing reconfiguring, enhancing from "Cyborology: Constructing the Knowledge Of Cybernetic Organisms." (Gray, C., Mentor, S., Figueroa-Sarriera, H. J, 1995)

Cyborgs are polymorphic and they presently exist, wondering among us. They are not visibly different from humans in part because these technologies have just been developed, in part because we are not trained to see how posthuman arises. Their birth, I argue, alters the core of medicine from disease containment and death assessment to enhancement of function and image, to transgression of previous bounds with regard to space and oceanic travel, but not limited by them. I delineate the main line of reasoning with regard to how cyborgs, as postmodern/posthuman products of medicine, make visible the shift in the construction of medical bodies, technologies, and objectives. I will briefly determine my main concerns in each section.

1. In the *Birth Of The Clinic*, Foucault[2] has demonstrated how medicine became a system of knowledge when it was able to define its objective as the preservation of life in opposition to its end or bound death. Illness was constructed as malfunctioning life that needed to be deciphered, and death was conceived as the ultimate/ inevitable course of life not only of illness. Consequently, medicine understood its object: life as bounded by death. Today the bound of medicine is no longer death (a "natural" constraint that took the form of an *Absolute*) since it can be indefinitely circumvented by technology. Rather, the present bound of medical competence is the invention of technologies that can help sustain high degrees of livability not only bypass death in the face of illness (an artificially projected and variable constraint). Historically, technological innovations have affected the way medical questions are asked, how problems have been defined, what objectives are formulated and how solutions, cures, treatments have been investigated; consequently, it is key to highlight the relation of technology to the formulation of medical concepts of cure and disease through out recent time. I will deal with the example of *Tuberculosis* at the turn of the century and compare it with the AIDS epidemic. I will eventually situate AIDS to be on the limits of present political and medical institutions of surveillance as a syndrome that does not have at present a cure because of the ways in which it challenges the conceptualization of immunity politically, historically, and epidemiologically.

As techno-biological hybrids, cyborgs become the second key features of my analysis in that they embody the medical desire for ultimate performances and boundary crossing. So I will finally deal with the likelihood of an HIV+ cyborg at the juncture where the objective of medical

---

[2] Foucault has been criticized by historians in his lack of attention to detail and his eagerness to produce general interpretive schema. For example, Roy Porter claims that there was no great confinement of the mentally ill in Britain, and that the mentally ill were separated from other deviants. (Porter, R., 1995) Roy Porter, thus, questions the constitution of the category of the unthought that runs through out Foucault's Madness And Civilization. Many criticisms have been produced with regard to Foucault's work, Birth of the Clinic, most notably those published in the special issue of The Journal Of Medicine and Philosophy, devoted to Michel Foucault And The Philosophy Of Medicine. He has also been critiqued by some Feminists for his lack of attention to issues of Gender: examples abound (a collection of essays Up Against Foucault would be a good place to start). However, I feel that his approach merits close attention especially in his attempt to unravel the relation of power/ knowledge (objectivity/ subjectivity) and the constitution of disciplinary borders (that construct distinct disciplines: Medicine proper) that so many critics attribute to him as a fault. The project of a more Philosophical History or a Historical Philosophy is not new. It has its roots in both Kant and Hegel.

knowledge to invent technological cures that enhance livability is confronted with the limit of current medical conceptual frames: AIDS. As a result, AIDS research is a particular frontier where technologies are constantly invented to contain its effects. It is, thus, crucial to understand how cyborgs pretend to or may actually offer a solution to the medical impasse in the face of an epidemic, how indeed they are born on the current medical bounds as its present proper objects. At least they embody the will of medico-political institutions to surveil and restrain diseased bodies even if they have to ultimately be immobilized and hooked up to life-sustaining machines. The founding of the hospital/ clinic has been quintessential in the making of modern medicine. Cyborgs, however, do mark the end of the clinic in that surveilling technologies will continually be incorporated so that the resulting beings can no longer be termed human and are hybrids. The present will to hyper-surveil bodies in ultra-technological medical states marks moments of rupture were what follows cannot resemble previous forms, yet still may have been conceived as a monster or deamon in fictional representations.

2. I attempt to establish how cyborgs are the figures that can survive post-modern hypercritiques although I am weary of the cyborgic emancipatory potential. I wish to help construct a post-gender, anti-racist, post-colonial, meta-class, global world, but I realize that cyborgs cannot possibly offer a solution to all the present social ills: notably the ones that relate to class and poverty in their various manifestations in terms of gender, race, first/ third world. Technologies destabilize notions of the natural as ground/ bound, yet they are already determined by these categories as a function of class, so it becomes clear they are assured to reproduce them in certain ways. Therefore, strategies of resistance need to be set in motion to guarantee that technologies are not restricted by the interest of a technocratic elite, that boundaries between the haves and the have nots are not stabilized, crystallized in distinctive oppositions or antagonisms, which should be constantly challenged. Cyborgic figures may transgress the present medico-political impasse because they subvert previous natural limits such as death and detach nature from the *Absolute* ground that scientific discourse has placed it.

Nevertheless, economic and political factors that are presently operating, still are likely to strategically reproduced as a bound the advantage they have not as an explicit ideology of the nationalist, racist, sexist, homophobic variety (since they are constantly deconstructed and are too visible), but an implicit one as it pertains to class and opportunity. I, thus, will delineate the ways in which technology is interested by envisioning the construction of a medical cyberspace as the field where cyborgs do not roam free (enlightenment ideal), but are plugged in and hyper-supervised. As such, identities and the institutions that support them will change to accommodate the ways in which cyborgs interact and constitute a place, a forum where public/ private/ personal is actively re-negotiated, where the contours of the body/ subject/ patient are re-written, where notions of space/ location/ confinement, nation/ state/ institution as local implode.

It is clear that cyborgic technologies have the potential to radically alter the basis of everyday life what is considered home/ work, inside/ outside, what is the vary basis of interaction between institutions/ individuals/ bodies, how communities, and collaborative identities are established, even the vary basis of bodily reproduction with the revolution of birth-tech. Medicine has facilitated the connection between individuals and bodies through the regulations required to contain disease. When the notions of disease and body change due to novel technologies, then the concept of self utilized by the nation/ state that has to implement public health policies will also change. I locate, through the examples of Tuberculosis and AIDS, how such medical identities come into being, and how the qualifications of experts tend to dissociate themselves from the diseased individuals in a sense blaming them for their predicament. Cyberspace, thus, can expose the ways in which medical identities have been constituted to serve specific interests under the guise of scientific, objective universality, and the preservation of certain forms of power/ knowledge. Power has been always secured upon a clear, self-evident, universal, *a priori* ground that could establish coherent identities and relations of dominance. I demonstrate how that is no longer possible, desirable, or viable in the present situation, how the structure of power/ knowledge will have to radically change to what I term *power sharing structures of governmentality.*

3. It is important to understand that cyborgs are born not only on the frontier of medical knowledge, but also at the point where human and natural sciences via engineering meet. This location undermines the primary opposition of living and artifact that is at the basis of scientific mediation and results in the linguistic distinction between subject/ object, between active/ passive modalities. The bio-medical sphere is where such a meeting has its most radical and controversial applications from simple devices that enhance function to the potential of genetically engineering future posthuman generations. It is meaningful to view the effects of expert-technologies not as totalizing, but rather as contested and contingent because perfect control and total knowledges have proven to be fallible and even dangerous myths of the modernist variety. Here I set out to map the medical field in view of the changes to bodies, technologies, and objectives that I established to have been taking place. The main site of conceptual rehashing is the clinic as a place of bodily enclosure. Postmodernities as articulated through technological innovations have managed to implode the modern sense of enclosure whether that is considered self, home, work, body, clinic.

The result is an unsettling of the categorical split between private/ public and a problematization of the conceptions of rights that are founded upon that very distinction. If in cyberspace one can no longer talk about private/ public but rather of more or less secure information, and if private/ public is stripped down to mediation of information flows and accessibility, then it is disrobed of the enlightenment rhetoric that has found it as the privileged site for the construction of the citizen/ patient/ subject. It is possible, then, to conceive of medicine without clinics and doctors, a medicine interested in developing prosthetic devices to deliver to the posthuman market upon demand. Therefore, the frontier of bioengineering is centered upon diagnostic technologies that will eventually be incorporated within the body to monitor its state. The cyber-preceptors have the potential to replace the doctor as practitioner, leaving open the space for experts to map out the field of knowledge. The final, thus, frontier would be to incorporate the expert/ researcher with prosthetic artificial intelligence that would allow for greater memory banks, and more effective molding of facts to conceptually re-map the knowledge field in more advanced and systematic ways.

4. It is critical not to become caught up in the future possibilities and forget what we are creating in the process and at what cost. Hence, I will address the political implications and ironic consequences of the cyborg solution. I lay down the crucial criticisms to scientific universalism and triumphalism to reveal how we can construct an alternative vision that allows for greater flexibility of conception, and circumvents the totalizing of enlightenment rhetorical narratives. I attempt to delineate how cyborgs can be constructed as postmodern partially determined subjects and objects, how they can be the basis for collaborative identifications, and how they contest the process of medicalization in modern states. It is meaningful to exploit the distinction between partial and unfinished: as such, the work of knowledge will always be unfinished and its subject/object partial. The dynamic created from this separation is what will move us towards new directions, to establish a conceptual grid for our thought process. *Differences* and *Collaborations* should be grasped as the strings, which weave together our thought not through an enforced consensus, but through the process of unfolding in various speeds and directions.

It is incisive to understand that the unfoldings of our thought does not need to follow the path past/present/ future, before/ during/ after in a sequential fashion that has focused upon the establishment of the causal event as legitimate and central. Rather, it is a choreographed interplay of diversity and collaboration, between figure and ground that yields the direction of argument towards novel approaches, that redefines the relation of limits and bounds, agency and thought not through a negative dichotomy of self/ other, but through a continual re- evaluation of differences. The direction and speed of argument, thus, need to break out of a linear/ causal mode that has been essential in a Newtonian/ Cartesian construction of space to show how the movement of discussion does not need to be unidimensional and singular. Singularity seems to be always coerced. CyberFeminisms have attempted to establish an umbrella of critiques vis a vis enlightenment ideals of progress and science. It is significant to understand how they can offer resolution to the impasse produced by modernity in the face of postmodern critiques.

In this thesis, cyborgs both mythos and real are examined alongside medical and political institutions in the face of crisis whether that crisis is an effect of disease or technological innovation. The goal is to raise awareness of the operations of medical and political institutions and the directions that trends are taking, so checks can be set in place to ensure an ethical outcome. Without awareness little hope can be left for critique and resistance to play a role in the shaping of the future.

I. The Technical Cure For Mortality As The Ultimate Medical Performance

> *What is being set in place here is, in effect, the immortality of the species in real time. We long ago stopped believing in the immortality of the soul, a deferred immortality. We no longer believe in that immortality which assumed a transcending of the end, an intense investment in the finalities of the beyond and a symbolic elaboration of death. What we want is the immediate realization of immortality by all possible means. (Baudrillard, 1994: 89-90)*

Medicine is the expertise that determines the state of our bodies in fitness, illness, and death though its practices, its institutions of accreditation, its suggested policies for maintaining public health, and its strategies for prescribing and discovering the appropriate cures. The responsibility of medicine has been to diagnose the disease of ill bodies and to prescribe remedies that sustain functionality at the minimum of cost. (Foucault, 1994) Medicine has thus provided the means for enlightened societies to assist the poor/ misfortunate. Or rather as class and race analysis illustrate, medicine has historically secured the rich/white in their attempt to contain illness in the poor/ black and to experiment on them so that treatments for diseases that might also plague the rich/ white can be invented. (Foucault, 1994/ Savitt, 1978) As labor demands increased with the industrialization of society, the necessity for a public health revolution has been pivotal in maintaining the work force and consequently economic growth as in the example of the tuberculosis epidemic in eighteen century England (Porter, R., 1992a) and Europe. Medicine, then, has become more scientific (read reliable), so it has been connected with liberal state policy not simply to preserve health standards, but also a healthy economy, and its goals has included observing existing health habits, establishing what remedies are the most effective, and making sure that the "right" kinds of medicine have been practiced. (Porter, R., 1992a)

The objectives of Enlightenment medicine are in some regards still valid since malady has not vanished as the illusion of a disease free society had projected. However, medicine has become complicated by the advent of illnesses that at present do not have a cure, like AIDS, by the increasing fervor to map the human genome and to ascribe genetic causes or cures to diseases, and by the demands of modern warfare that forges human bodies beyond their genetic makeup in environments that are unfamiliar like the depths of the sea or outer-space travel. Cyborgs (short for *cyber*netic[3] *org*anisms) are thus constructed by the addition of technical, bio-technical, genetic, or chemical devices to our bodies in order to control and regulate unwanted or unnecessary bodily functions in new and potentially unwelcoming environments or circumstances.

---

[3] Cybernetics as a term was introduced by Norbert Wiener from the Greek word κυβερνητική that means the art of governing. The first half of cybernetics: "cyber" is used to "represent the possibilities of travel and existence in the new space of computer networks, a space, it is argued, that must be negotiated by the human mind in new kinds of ways." (Sandoval, 1995: 420n6)

(Clynes and Kline, 1995) Cyborgs have clear military implications at their conception. Nevertheless, cyborgs can offer a vehicle through which a better understanding of postmodern bodies, diseases, knowledges, and ethics is located because they are contested hybrids where what is and what might be join in fantasy, ideality, and projected reality. They, as illegitimate hybrids, do mark for some the birth of a postgender, postcolonial, and even metaracist world (Haraway, 1992), and for others, indicate the violent corruption or collapse of the state giving way to or colliding with all powerful multinational corporations as in comic book representations (Oehlert, 1995). Beyond these utopic or dystropic visions, I will determine how cyborgs are the product of medical technologies and knowledges even if they are heavily mediated by the military or the state, and their futures will be decided by the ways in which medical policy is formulated and by whom. Cyborgs embody the desire of capitalism for ultimate performances and the medical objective to preserve life at all costs and in all circumstances.

Cyborgs also denote a shift in medical objectives from surveilling diseased bodies to contain infections, preparing guidelines for maintaining public health standards, and inventing ways to treat illness, to modeling tailor-made prosthetics and procedures that enhance image or function (cosmetics, artificial limbs), designing technologies that monitor bodily performance through imaging technics (MRI, CAT, Ultrasound), and maintaining life (and thus the need for medical attention) at all costs. They attempt to materialize the medical promise of immortality, or rather a constant deferral or transgression of death through technical means. The questions remain at what cost, in whose benefit, and can medicine really deliver the fantasized control over bodies through their cyborgic transmutation. Cyborgic fantasies cover a rift in medicine: the differing aims of doctors and patients visible through its present failures, i.e., the AIDS epidemic or the current euthanasia debate as represented by Dr. Death, and they offer the promise of bodily integrity and immortality through technological prosthetics. The contours of medicine are defined by its bounds. Thus at the boundaries, the operations of medical and political institutions become visible. Their investments exposed by the public confrontation of differing interests, desires, wills, and the increasing discoursification of those conflicts. In my making out of the contours of postmodern medicine, I will mainly measure its cyborgic fantasies against the very real and sobering reality of the current AIDS epidemic to see for whom if indeed it is possible any longer for medicine to promise immortality. Cyborgs can, thus, be deemed as symptomatic of the current medical impasse.

Immortality is a medical promise and obsession. The question is in what state will bodies survive, at what degrees of livability since life functions can be indefinitely sustained mechanically. The desire that medical knowledge will one day be able to answer to death and prepare as projected today technical prosthetics for survival is reflected in the expectancy of bodies frozen in liquid nitrogen (*cryogenics*). They await the moment of their second awakening in full function (?) and with the will to play frozen *Lazarus* reborn to see the world anew. Maybe by then medicine would have mastered the reversibility of cell decay or at least legitimized cloning technics, so that the current methods of social regeneration through reproduction would appear archaic. Underwriting this fantasy of complete mastery and competence is a medical failure: the powerlessness in the confrontation with the AIDS epidemic that damages the very basis of our immunity where total immunity would approximate immortality. Therefore, it is not an accident that the desire for immortality as proclaimed through the dreams of frozen bodies have risen contemporaneously with the challenge of the epidemic as if the desire for the cure has projected itself into the proclamation of full mastery.

In order to figure out how the relation of medical knowledge (as a limit) to death (as a bound) has altered, it is necessary to map out the changes in the notions of death and disease through technological innovation, so that shifts in conception can become visible by the birth of cyborgs. With the enclosure of sick bodies within the hospital, the scene of death has been increasingly enclosed and infused with experimental technologies and techniques. Medicine, then, has become more technologically mediated, so the definitions of death and disease have altered in order to fit the novel conditions that persons who are terminally ill or in a coma. A shift can be noticed from a medicine that read the signs of death to a medicine that has determined the cause of death and eventually a medicine that has maintained life technologically to provide alternate or experimental treatments. Presently, the distinctions of life and death have become unclear and defined by the notion of minimal brain function. (Hogle, 1995) The haziness in the distinction between life and death is portrayed by the Stengl's 1988 film *I Take Care Of Dead Patients* that "explores caregivers' feelings about this work, including doubts that the patient is dead or irreversibly dead." (Hogle, 1995: 212) Especially when these bodies may have spinal reflexes: "the arms may rise, eyes may open, or other parts might move spontaneously, making the person appear alive." (Hogle, 1995: 212)

Death is marked by an irreversible brain wave pattern that allows the doctor ethically and legally to unplug the patient. As a result, euthanasia has become an ethical question: the debate whether or not the patient has the right to unplug him/herself. (Crigger, 1993) The last border between life and death has shifted from the lungs and heart to the brain paralleling the frontiers of medical knowledge. Disputes, over whether or not a sustained heart beat should be defined as a sign of life, have been intense especially in countries like Japan where only recently the concept of brain death is accepted. (Hogle, 1995) I will demonstrate how the definitions/models of death and disease have adjusted with the development of the clinic and with increased mediation by technology, how in the face of epidemics (Tuberculosis/ AIDS) medicine in crisis has confined the diseased body to establish expert discourses. The medical enclosure is where the body is infused with information and technology, is where cyborgs are born. Cyborgs establish medical bounds and limits that are re-negotiated since the concept of observation needs to be re-determined in terms of simulation-tech. I will show how AIDS clearly demarks a limit of medical knowledge (in terms of the operations of the immune system), and how cyborgs as mythos may obscure this limit by establishing themselves as a convenient solution to the present impasse. Finally, I will measure cyborgic dreams of immortality and how they are always socially determined by looking at the likelihood of cyborgian AIDS patient.

1. Shifting Notions Of Death And Disease Under An Epidemic Crisis Through The Lens of Medical-Technologies.

The formalization of medicine as a discipline occurred when it was able to codify its own failures and shortcomings, when it described the accident of death as rooted in the body, when it opened up corpses to see how the inevitability transpired, when it was able to describe at what precise point death overtook life. (Foucault, 1994) Medicine never took responsibility for the inevitability of death, but emphasized its signs, and denuded death from its mystery. The goal of medicine was to continually delay the "natural" bound of death in the name of life and the growing medical respectability. With the making of the clinic/ hospital into the proper site of medical endeavors, and with the scientifization of its knowledge, medicine was utilized by the state to surveil the habits of its subjects and curb public ignorance that was viewed as pathogenic and infectious to the social body. (Porter, R., 1992b) Medicine, thus, offered its concept of diseased body as linked to patient identity to the state, which was then able to establish health guidelines for the circulation of bodies and fluids. Thus, patient identity was connected to citizenship status. The discourse on immigration that surveils national boarders, presently, has been determined on the basis of medical and economic policies.

It has been of key political importance for medical expertise to codify how death/ disease occurred or was transmitted, and how it could be dealt with, inscribed in symbolic discourse to maintain order. Depictions of the state as an organic body have begun with Hobbes (1651). As a result, disease has been represented as pathogenic to the whole social body, and its course was thought to be contained though an identification and structuring in terms of a taxonomic order. Death and the signs of morbidity became established by external physical marks, by listening to life histories, which have been the central features of the ritual interaction between doctors and diseased bodies, so that the potential origins of diseases could be discovered and controlled. (Bynum & Porter, 1993) Thus, medicine has been confined to the discourse of symptoms that doctors classified through patients' descriptions, attempting to determine the causes of illness and to decipher the body real. (Porter, R., 1993) The contrast between the relation of doctors to live or dead bodies can illumine how medicine has conceived its objects and goals. Consequently, it is important to mark how the relation of doctor to live or dead patient has changed with increased technologization. A clear contrast in the relation between doctor and body is evident with the acceptance of dissection, briefly sketched from the 17th century.

The contact of doctor/ patient could be described as personal before the inevitability of death. Afterwards the life-history of the person and the doctor's sensing of the patient's condition became less personal and standardized, foreshadowing the violence of dissection performed on cadavers. Robert Burton's *The Anatomy of Melancholy* (published in 1621) has established how medical dissection became the model for the methods of partitioning evident in the pre-scientific cultural imagination. (Sawday, 1995) But partitioning dead bodies had been viewed as a taboo, so doctors sought then, guarded with a scalpel and a mirror, to violate (partition) the bodies of marginal members: "the criminal, the poor, the insane, suicides, orphans, even simply 'strangers.'" (Sawday, 1995: 3) The medical gaze eventually was constructed by this anatomical dissecting and looking. The history of anatomic illustration has determines how the cadavers were skinned to display more clearly the secrets held in the "truth" of human bodies. (Kemp, 1993) The evolution of these illustrations and their acceptance in anatomic textbooks has suggested that in later years the text became subordinated to the image that was initially manipulated so that the reader could see what the author/ authority intended. Two main modes of illustration evolved a simple portrait that attempted to give the object in full detail or a representational object, which was conceived in the imagination and illustrated the idea behind the picture. (Kemp, 1993) So far medical technologies were in infant form. They included illustrations, dissection, standardized viewing or sensing, and textual accounts of the encounter between cadavers and physicians while the discourse of live patient/ doctor retained the form of an informal verbal account.

The encounter of live patient/ physician was highly irregular. It had been up to doctors to perceive how they would conduct themselves. Their contacts with live patients tended to have the abstract form of an oral account: the patient's descriptions of his/ her condition. It was not until the Victorian age that physical examination was developed and accepted as a norm. (Porter, R., 1993) Before the invention of the stethoscope the doctor was reluctant to directly sense the sick body before death (except for surgeons), then physical contact became standard practice. (Porter, R., 1993) Eventually, live bodies were constructed as the direct objects of observation as technologies or methods were invented to help assess their condition. Touch had to be purified of its sexual connotations for it to be accredited as a part of the physical examination (Porter, R., 1993), since touch was always associated with sexuality and disease (Gilman, 1993). The scientifization of medicine brought the scene of death behind the hospital or clinic walls. There the scene of death became increasingly mediated by medical knowledge and technology. The exact arrangement of the medical scene in the hospital and the elimination of outside influences allowed medical scientists to determine the course of illnesses and to generalize patterns of disease with a course towards death. (Foucault, 1995) Mapping the exact path of malady was central in distinguishing between species of disease and prescribing the proper cure. Opening up corpses allowed the observant doctor to ascertain the exact failure that promoted death and to demark at point at which it had occurred. Death was viewed as the ultimate course of most illnesses, but not necessary a function of illness itself. Illness was conceived as malfunctioning life whereas death was viewed as the ultimate bound of that malfunction. (Foucault, 1994).

The revolution of surgical method noted in the decade 1879-1886 marked the shift from heroic practice of medicine that required a leap of faith from doctors and patients to prescribe and follow treatments such as "blistering, bleeding and purging." (Brieger, 1993: 226), to a medicine that was more scientific, and able to determine the patient's illness through instrumental means. Surgery has been perhaps the most intrusive medical technique to date and it became more acceptable when anti-inflammation strategies were discovered and standardized along with diagnostic technologies. The desire of the surgeons to know and to gaze at the interior of sick bodies, to detect and cure malfunction, was constructed in opposition to patients' desires who "through pain [could] mask or conceal their interior discomfort, by allowing no visible sign to escape onto the exterior. " (Sawday, 1995: 12) The surgeon, thus, has attempted to find methods to denude the body and expose its inoperative interiority to medical knowledge and technics. The surgical gaze pried into the live and diseased body penetrating its skinned enclosure, and displaying the material base of malfunction that was novel to the standard verbal basis of doctor-patient interplay.

Late 19th century surgery quickly distanced itself from knifemen who opened up patients too easily. (Brieger, 1993) Surgery was aided by the establishment of hospitals and laboratories where standardized surgical practice occurred and was nourished by the revolution in diagnostic technology and instrumentation. The end of the 19th century brought on arguments as to whether or not "instruments of precision actually provided the practitioner with new and useful data as advocates claimed as well as on the extent to which diagnostic instruments intruded upon the doctor-patient relationship, shifting the focus from the patient to the disease." (Borell, 1993: 246) Instruments challenged the long held practice that technological tools had no place in medicine, that "the physician was to observe and question patients to gain diagnostic knowledge, not to poke and probe their bodies." (Reiser, 1993: 263) Diagnostic tests were developed to make medicine more exact. Medicine, thus, used technological and laboratory techniques to read the marks of the disease upon the physical body and understand the function of disease itself as a separate ontology that had a distinct biological form. Technological inventions in the last part of the 19th century included "the stethoscope, microscope, ofthalmoscope, and the thermometer" (Borell, 1993: 246) and were used to establish the form of disease as a virus or bacterium.

A pivotal point for surgery in America was the establishment of the Johns Hopkins Hospital that was connected to the University and its medical school, which fostered the laboratory approach to the problems of the surgeon. (Brieger, 1993) The connection of a hospital to the University was important in connecting students with novel laboratory methods and has served as a model of medical institutions to date. Technology was thus introduced as a means to permeate with and read from the body its information. Technologies have modified the initial setting of the doctor-patient relation from an oral account to a data set. By the turn of the century, instrumental readings of disease represented the exactness of laboratory science and appealed to the scientifization of medical knowledge. (Borell, 1993) Instruments initially developed as forms of "sensory penetration, while challenging the body's boundaries, none the less [left] the actual, physical boundary intact [unlike surgery that was more traumatic]." (Logan, 1991:202) The problem then became how to standardize instruments so that variations in data would be reduced. (Borell, 1993) Medical practice manuals established as a pretense for increased technologization of medicine the limitations of human perception. The expectation of the medical techno-reformers was to invent instrumental capacities apt to transgress these human sensory limitations. (Borell, 1993) They established instrumental technologies to be on the bound of medical perception not necessarily of medical knowledge.

With the advent of laboratory techniques in medicine, there has been a re-conception of what disease could be, and how it can be treated. (Cunningham, 1992) The years of radical technological reform in medicine have been contemporary to the rise of *tuberculosis* in epidemic proportions all throughout Europe and America at the end of the 19th century. The conceptions of illness/ health beginning with 17th century have been replaced by a germ-theory of disease. The conception of a disease agent has provided grounds for the construction of diseased patienthood. Thus, medicine through this conception of patient identity has set the groundwork for the birth of individual as an identity utilized in the politics of infected bodies as culminating in tuberculosis 19th century/ AIDS 20th century.

Before the Enlightenment, medicine was concerned with preserving a state of health as established through ancient tradition. (Foucault, 1988) When John Donne fell ill, he noted that "We study Health and we deliberate upon our meats and drink and Ayre and exercises, and we hew, and wee polish every stone, that goes to that building; and so our Health is a long & regular work; but in a minute a Cannon batters all, overthrows all, demolishes all; a sickness unprevented for all our diligence, unsuspected for all our curiositie; nay undeserved, if we consider only disorder, summons us, seizes us, possesses us, destroyes us in an instant" (Donne: 7) The vulnerability of the best health regimen to debilitating illness was common because medicine could only articulate the signs of illness to determine the disease by a process of elimination, and not by identifying the disease itself. At moments of illness, the body became isolated "'it' had begun to exist as distinct from 'we'" (Sawday, 1995: 35)

Medical surveillance of diseased bodies was pivotal in identifying the body with the individual enclosed in the home and later the hospital. With the laboratory revolution, medicine became able not only to identify the sick body with a particular disease-description that might fit the symptoms, but actually identify the disease as a distinct species, having a form of its own under the microscope. For example, the fact that *Bacillus Pestis* caused the bubonic plague was discovered, "and of course the presence of B. pestis can only be established in the laboratory, using all the proper tests." (Cunningham, 1993, 218) A clear example of the construction of disease in the early modern era is *Tuberculosis* whose infecting agent was located in 1882 by Koch, and thus termed the Koch bacillus or *microbictirium tuberculosis*, along with the inoculability of the disease as demonstrated by Vilemin in 1865. (Barnes, 1995)

The *tuberculosis* epidemic shows how technologies and in particular the development of germ-theory, as related to the discovery of the microscope, altered the ways that the TB epidemic was confronted by policy makers. During the pre-germ theory years in France, many causes were supposed to be at the basis of the rise of tuberculosis such as "filth, stench, and overcrowding" (Barnes, 1995:25) or the "sorrowful passions" as supposed by René-Théophile-Hacinthe Laënnec in 1826 40 years before he invented the stethoscope. (Barnes, 1995) In these pre-germ theory years, the disease was viewed in terms of a social phenomenon, and an effect of urbanization. As a result, the early hygienists conceived of mortality as a social disease that was determined by lifestyle. Villermé (the leading figure of "the party of hygiene") illustrated how social statues could produce relative immunity to the disease, plainly put: "the poor were sicker and died earlier than the rich." (Barnes, 1995: 31) Villermé was able to reject several factors that had been considered as key to the contagious nature of tuberculosis. Through epidemiological and statistical analysis, he rejected "climate, soil drainage, water supply, miasmatic filth, altitude, wind patterns" (Barns, 1995: 32) as key factors. In fact, he was able to match nearly exactly the mortality rate with the inverse rank of wealth.

The socio-epidemiological argument failed to take into account the innovations in medical technics that were occurring at the time, and continued to regard problematic the establishment of the contagious status of tuberculosis through the discovery of an infecting agent. Pidoux's polemic against Villemin's demonstration has established how conceptual frames need to be kept in flux and not fixated on distinct concepts. The main line of health policy to address the overcrowding of slum-houses was kept in tact despite the change in the conceptual frame with regard to the nature of the disease. Pidoux's argument displayed the resistance of old medicine to the rise of experimental and laboratory technics. (Barnes, 1995) After the identification of the consumption germ, efforts were made to minimize contagion through a war on tuberculosis, and spiting was targeted as the main enemy along with physical contact. (Barnes, 1995) "The resulting bacillophobia turned casual passerby into suspects, and patients into potentially murderous coughers and spitters." (Barnes, 1995) The result was to confine visibly sick patients into sanatoriums. The making of sanatoriums as the places where consumption has been contained as not necessarily a means of curing it, but minimizing its contagious character was a generalized practice at the turn of the century in both Europe and America.

The making of the modern patient could be connected with the practice of confinement in sanatoriums. It has been deemed necessary "to confine anyone found 'liable to jeopardize the health of others.'" (Rothman, 1994: 191) Almost exclusively the practice of confinement has been exercised "against the vagrant, the poor, and the immigrant." (Rothman, 1994:192) Even though the numbers of persons confined has not been extremely large, the interplay of political and medical institutions with notions of illness and risk formed the ground upon which infected individuals lost their autonomy. Therefore, marginal forms of identity have arisen in times of uncertainty to contain perceived risk. Yet the effects of scapegoating policies (other than appeasing the fears of the main stream public) has had a minimal if no impact on the course of overall tuberculosis infection. The fear of mandatory confinement of persons that have been determined to be HIV+, thus, can be justified, and has arisen as a possibility in the early years of the epidemic. However, such path has not been chosen probably due to the fact that HIV is not contagious but infectious, and that the group mainly targeted by such policies (gay men) have been politically organized, and could influence the course of policies. Clearly, confinement has not minimized the numbers of persons dying from TB in advance societies at the turn of the century.

The fact that the infecting agent of tuberculosis was determined, set up expectations that a cure could have been invented; however this confidence has proven to be illusive since tuberculosis deaths have not vanished, but have faded away in "developed" countries, affecting mainly patients with deficient immunities such as AIDS patients. The sanatorium has eclipsed as a place of "cure"; nevertheless, its occurrence establishes the interpermeation of medical and political institutions in moments of crisis, at the face of a contagious epidemic, and the ways in which patient identities were determined, how they have related to notions of norm, and how they have established, through default, clusters of immunity as accessed by the privilege to knowledge and information about the disease and the means of infection. The sanatorium was conceived upon the hospital-model, and can be seen today in the milder form of the AIDS ward. However, the confinement in such setting has not been mandatory. The determination of the hospital as a place of cure found its ultimate deduction to the sanatorium as a place of hygienic surveillance and treatment: its emergence was tied up with the promise of laboratory science and observation.

Medicine has been unable to fulfill the desire for a cure or treatment for tuberculosis, which illustrates how the medical conception of disease, and immunity have been under construction. Research on human immune system, and how it is said to operate have intensified lately in the face of the AIDS epidemic. The development of the conceptual models of immunity also have been established in the mid to late 20th century, and those efforts have intensified with the advent of HIV. During the early years of the epidemic, the connections of medical and political discourses have been illustrated by the portrayal of immunity as military defense as shown by *Time* magazine in 1984, which has represented HIV as an "invasion." The virus has been "imagined as a tank, and the viruses ready for export from expropriated cells are lined up as tanks ready to continue their advance on the body as a productive force." (Haraway, 1988: 31) *Star war* depictions of the immune system has prevailed in the 80s since a need for political espousal of the defense program can be discerned so the program has been connected with a newly established vulnerability that raided the United States imagination.

Inspite of the potential political benefit, which has accrued by the representation of HIV as an invasion, *Star War* representations illumine how military notions of vulnerability to attack have been structured in parallel to our sense of vulnerability to disease. It is certain that the medical-military complex has been keen on its development of technologies: cyborgs being another example. The development of technologies, as means of sensory penetration, as methods of establishing the types of disease or enemy, and as central to developing cures or counter strategies, have appealed to the militaristic and popular imaginations, and as such defense technologies are conceptualized through the parallel of immune system discourse and the military. This parallel between immunity and defense rhetoric indicates how the state is conceptualized as an organic totality. Technology poses as an answer to both immunologic and defense problems. Such privileged position needs to be problematized.

I have determined how medical sciences have been opposed to the use of tools, which stands in clear contrast to the present hyper-dependence upon instrumental technologies as diagnostic (sensory-penetration) devices. The advent of the laboratory has promoted the increased acceptance of the use of newly established technics to decipher the disease of the body, and the relation of the doctor-patient shifted to fit the new order of things, where the life history became subordinate to the techno-medical probing. The increased technological probing of medicine, and the construction of the medical gaze as the analytical, partitioning gaze of the anatomist demonstrates how the diagnostically examined live body (and not the account of the individual) is at the center of medical inquiry. Thus, the demands of furthering medical knowledge have legitimized the increased surveillance of the live body and its habits, and the invention/ development of monitoring technologies as made available by the hospital. Thus, Foucault's parallel between the prison and the hospital as materializations of panopticon vision: the desire to constantly observe, is justified whether the submission to the gaze is voluntary, internalized, or enforced.

The submission to surveillance is born out of the pains of an incurable disease, the memory of calamity (a natural disaster, criminality, war), and the fear such adversity might occur at any moment. The appeal of surveillance becomes the reduction of risk (or rather a rationalization of risk) so that unknown factors can be contained, so that "the plague is [always] met by order; its function is to sort out every possible confusion: that of disease, which is transmitted when bodies are mixed together; that of evil, which is increased when fear and death overcome prohibitions." (Foucault, 1979: 197) Medical and political institutions, therefore, are intertwined through the informed, expert gaze that sees and pretends to know how to lay down the rules to avoid these catastrophes: "It lays down for each individual his [/her] place, his[/her] body, his [/her] disease and his [/her] death, his [/her] well-being, by means of an omnipotent and omnipresent power that subdivides itself in a regular, uninterrupted way even to the ultimate determination of the individual, of what characterizes him [/her], of what belongs to him [/her], of what happens to him [/her]." (Foucault, 1979: 197)

Medical intrusion (through diagnostic devices) has been extended beyond the bodily enclosure as a totality, which it has defined as a site of its operation, to the function, determination, and improvement of body parts. This fragmentation of bodily totality is evident in the example of "dead" bodies suitable for organ donation. (Hogle, 1995) Through the example of organ donation one can see how each part of the body dies/ terminates at a different time, defining a window of opportunity when organs from "dead" persons may be used as transplants. (Hogle, 1995) This fragmentation of bodily totality has been aided by imaging technology that can isolate organs to determine the functions and operation of various parts, which now can be even viewed live as they perform in bodies. Imaging tech (visionics) has provided the needed control over live versus dead bodies, which had been absent in the interaction of doctors and patients to enable better prevention and diagnosis. Concepts of live vs. dead body have been challenged by the more specified definition of termination: from the ultimate, possible end to a debilitating condition that may not have caused it, to a failure of a particular life sustaining function increasingly supported by technology. Death (termination) has become localized: heart failure, lung collapse, brain death, and technical devices have been developed and introduced to maintain vital functions of an ever more corrupted and diseased body. The medical game has now centered on the contours of its previous natural bound: death, and has figured out how to transgress it, and to preserve life via technology.

Technological devices have become indispensable in the preservation of life functions, so now technical devices are required to determine if and when the minimal limit of livability has been crossed, if life has yielded to death, and if it is ethical to take a body off the life supporting mechanisms. The containment of the diseased body in the hospital and its dependence upon technology has produced the cyborg, at once hyper-supervised, plugged in, and immobilized. The question remains are such surveillance technologies able to provide immunity from disease? The case of the sanatorium testifies otherwise. In fact, one can relate the overcoming of tuberculosis in "advanced" societies as an effect of the rising economic status of the whole society, an argument proposed both by Barnes in *The Making of A Social Disease*, and noted by Bynum at the end of his book on *Science and the practice of Medicine In the Nineteenth Century*. Surveillance (observation and discoursification), however, as Foucault noted is the pretext for the generation of expert knowledge not a cure; it enables the lucid construction of objects of study as embodied in distinct others, stabilizing the bounds of these concrete objects, as they are always socially and politically mediated, and concealing the limits of the expert discourse to resolve the problem that served as the pretext of observation. It is important to keep in check the aims of expert discourses to dissolve the fixation upon an absolute object or the pretension of total control or perception.

The reliability or fallibility of hi-tech control and surveillance tactics today can be plotted through the responses towards the AIDS epidemic. AIDS establishes a place for potential cyborgic resistance to medico-political imperatives (mandatory testing being a specific example). Technologies have permeated the body as an enclosure that stabilizes former medical formulations of patienthood, challenging its borders, so that the "bodily" can hardly be considered "private" i.e. the domain of individual, but "public," justifying an extension of the powers to monitor it more closely. The implosion of bodily boundaries is paralleled with the collapse of "private" and "public" spaces in hyperreal societies, and the denaturing of gendered identifications that these spaces had produced and mirrored. The challenge of postmodern institutions is to figure out how postmodern polysemic mirrors (computers) determine bounds and limits that might be simulations, and can serve as the basis for shape-lifter identities. These identities are constructed as resistant to the totalizing potentials of medico-political discourses in their modern creation.

Net-politics, hyper-relationships with self and others, cyber-responsibilities (collective and individual) need to be refurbished through partial and collaborative identifications. Through hyper-surveillance, which monitors the relations between virtual bodies and is already introduced in telematic systems,[4] medicine can figure out how to reshape its objectives and practices to account for the technologically altered landscape. Thus, virtuality is not unreality, but rather a simulation of the real, and a pure artifice, to virtualize would mean to make a simulation or a hyper-textualization of 'real' representations. Hyper-surveillance points to virtualization, not only of work, government, law, medicine, education, knowledge, but also disciplining and punishing: it is the realization of the hyperpanopticon society where everything appears to be visible, yet it remains radically invisible, and absent.

---

[4] Telematic systems (or societies) are distinguished by the fact that their "pragmatic mode of domination and control is the code" (Bogard, 1996: 11) which generates informed and informated spaces of diversity and is established through the combination of surveillance strategies and simulation that materialize the hyper*panopticon*.

The implosion of bodily boundaries illustrates the misrecognition in present identifications, and is produced by the continual demands upon permeating medico-political knowledge for infallible performances, and for the invention of technologies that transgress bounds that were conceived as definite: death. AIDS, thus, represents a limit to contemporary medicine that has chartered disease "in terms of pathological neuro-physiological processes that have natural (including emotional-mental and epidemiological) causes." (Rushing, 1995: 131) The current bound of medical objectives is not death per se since medicine has produced a living cadaver that gave birth (Hartouni, 1991), but technologies that can surpass the lapses of immunity in the form of incurable, transmutable illnesses that irreversibly corrupt our technologically supported bodies. AIDS, thus, challenges the borders of medico-political institutions, and their initial responses show bigotry and small mindedness in the face of an epidemic that lived up to our worst fears.

AIDS speeds up cell degeneration, causes dementia, and other debilitating unusual illnesses: contesting the promised dream of technological immortality; AIDS has revealed the costs (political and otherwise) in the failure to acknowledge new threats to human life, to determine sound public health policies. AIDS has not been dealt with early since it has been presumed to affect only marginal populations: gays, drug addicts, blacks (a hypothesis that has been proven faulty); and, since the free circulation of marginal persons can be checked, their loss deemed unimportant, and the rest of the population saved from the ills "they" propagated. Note that in the tuberculosis example the threat has been localized in the vagrants, immigrants, and marginalized members of society so that they needed to be contained, and certain practices or behaviors that they exhibited regulated (spitting, coughing).

I will display how our perceptions of illness and death are mediated by conflicting and contradictory social factors (Weeks, 1989:1), and how a disease like AIDS can re-figure medico-political institutions even though the constructing of new technologies justify increased surveillance and attempt to re-establish a stable unifying signifier that could be incorporated in the genealogy of power that is restructured in the face of radical change, chaos, and uncertainty. Major technological innovations also have occurred at the time of an epidemic when medicine is in crisis. This sheds a ray of hope that our expertise could develop strategies that would stop the growing death toll not only in advanced but poor societies as well.

2. AIDS: On The Limits Of Political And Medical Surveillance.

> *AIDS treatment activism does not depend on the us/them division in which the category of us is good, pure, natural, and human while the category them is bad, profit-seeking, contaminated, and cold-bloodedly technological. Rather, it has assembled out of available resources a complex conception of the body and a multilayered strategy for restoring it to health.(Treichler, 79)*

I have demonstrated how medical institutions have informed our concepts of body, disease, and death through increased technologization and surveillance, and how they have imploded the very constructions that once have been deemed indispensable, such as bodily totality, when conditions dictate. Cyborgs are established on the bounds of the physical: they are the product of increased surveillance of bodies and bodily functions through technical prosthetics and probing, which have undermined the supposed "naturalness" of the body and the essential distinctions between machine/ human/ animal. AIDS as a disease has raised the awareness of and the incentives for institutional observing of bodies for differing and conflicting reasons (fears of mandatory testing have been present from the beginning of the epidemic). The fight of AIDS patients for confidentiality and basic rights surely anticipates the struggles of cyborgs against more extensive types of bodily surveillance and intrusion. A projected fear? It will be determined in due course. Immunologic discourse (like cyborgs) appeals to military and medical imaginings. (Haraway, 1989) The analysis of immunologic discourse through the discourse on AIDS is a site of intricate and continual reconstruction, and displays how bodily immunity and livability translate into political and communal discourses of power/ knowledge. AIDS is not unique in this ability; tuberculosis is another such example. I utilize AIDS because there are many texts written on it presently, and thus it is at the center of debate.

AIDS (Advance Immune Deficiency Syndrome) initially has evaded medical probing. As a name, it is merely referential to the state of a person dying from a combination of unusual illnesses: AIDS related conditions or opportunistic infections, (Abrams, 1986) and a highly mutant virus (HIV) has been said to cause AIDS. The fact that AIDS has been associated with a virus detected in 1984 (Rushing, 1995) and a mechanism of how that virus attacks the human immune system has fueled the optimism that a cure for AIDS would soon be derived. So far such prospects have proved illusive. The best way to prevent the spreading of the virus has been to inform the public of the ways in which the disease can be transmitted, and how it can be prevented through "safer" practices (like safe sex, condoms, not sharing needles, not breast feeding). AIDS prevention strategies can be seen as community efforts to reestablish and protect the fallible immunity of bodies though guidelines of behavioral and sexual practices, coding "high risk" and "low risk" activities, constructing a discourse of immunologic restoration.

AIDS has primarily impacted the daily practice of individuals, who engage in "high risk" activities; of doctors, who handle risky body fluids; of policy makers, who lay down the rules of practice that alter the character of the disease, of identity, of relationships; of communities, who generally bear the task of information dissemination; and of activists, who attempt to inform politicians and the general public about the disease and the stereotyping of "high risk" lifestyles or individuals. Information accessing is the most important factor in keeping alive with AIDS, knowing what kinds of experimental treatments are available, and being able to participate in them. With the advent of the internet, online recourses have become essential in the lives of HIV+ persons, the access to such resources being sometimes free or charged. The relationship between information and immunity is central in understanding how one can remain healthy with HIV or not contract it. By the traditional use of information, the importance is placed upon reconstructing a problematic sense of immunity/ safety in times of epidemics/risks through an informatics of domination, establishing, thus, boarders between communities and "risky" individuals, prohibiting the free circulation of bodies, and maintaining conservative boundaries between classes, sexes, races, between normality and abnormality.

The use of information by activists, however, is to inform through a resistance to the stereotyping of medico-political institutions that have chosen to ignore or marginalize the risks of the epidemic. In both tuberculosis and AIDS, one can see how the marginalization of infection through a discourse on risk has been central to policy even if that implied the confinement of the most vulnerable individuals that may have not reduced the overall rate of infection. Thus, it is clear how power, information, and immunity are intertwined. Instead of a discourse on risk and stereotype, the medico- political game should figure out ways to transgress the traditional borders to information, and to inform not through bigotry, but through a will to preserve equity and autonomy of all persons. `Immunity [thus] can ... be conceived in terms of shared specificities [between individuals and communities/ activists and policy makers]; of the semi-permeable self able to engage with others (human and non-human, inner and outer) but always with finite consequences [determined by institutions]; of situated possibilities and impossibilities of individuation and identification; and of partial fusions and dangers" (Haraway, 1989:32). Immunity is what policy makers warrant by guidelines so that order can prevail over panic. The relations of doctors: sick bodies/ communities: patients can be restored through technologies and knowledges that prevent infection.

In the case of the AIDS, a resurgence of community activism (for example ACT UP) has been successful at times to reach out to its members, to influence policy makers, and the media. (Treichler, 1991) Making visible as a sufferer of AIDS celebrities like Rock Hudson or most recently Magic Johnson has sensitized the public to the risks of AIDS, to the discrimination towards AIDS patients, and has reached groups of people that may have disregarded information from other sources. The US government has been late to respond to AIDS because of the moralizing hysteria in the face of an epidemic. As a result, the sole defense to bodily immunities that initially prevailed had been to scapegoat and blame the victim, deviance, aliens, and any potentially, constructed Others from within or outside: Haitians, immigrants, blacks, homosexuals, prostitutes, drug users.... (Rushing, 1995) Later, the health policy debate in the US has tended to be articulated on the grounds of economics: it has been set between the US government and insurance companies, attempting to determine who is responsible for the financing of care to AIDS patients. The fact that economics shape health policies is unsettling, but it is clear how funding issues shape the responses to the epidemic, and what political line prevails even if that is coated as moralizing hysteria.

Thus, the claims of insurance companies to exclude persons that might be HIV+ or are coded to belong to a "high risk" group on the grounds of economic policy or marketing strategies have been unsuccessful since they have proven to be discriminatory and would leave Medicare or other charities to assume the cost of the epidemic. (Orr, 1990) A measure of political perceptions is the debates about what types of research or programs should be funded to construct expert knowledge about the epidemic. Not until recently, state funding for AIDS has been limited especially in areas of sociology, (Pollak, 1992) and mental health or counseling (Morin, 1986) because they have not been viewed as a valid means of "attacking" the epidemic to restore immunity for the global community. Since prevention has become essential to the deceleration of infection rates among "high risk" groups, such research has been deemed more appropriate. AIDS activism and awareness raising have placed pressure on policy makers to make more efforts to approach persons with "high risk" lifestyles avoiding, however, the stigmatization of such groups.

From the beginning of the epidemic people in "high risk" groups have been stigmatized and equated with the disease in the case of gay men: the epidemic has been named GRID (gay related immune deficiency), (Shilts, 1987) or in the case of blacks: the representations of AIDS threats in posters associated them again with touch, skin, sex, disease, and death. (Gilman, 1993) The history of the AIDS epidemic illumines how social mechanisms interact in the formation of an Other that is scapegoated for the fallibilities of systemic responses to collective info-immunologic threats towards the bio-social body. The African and non-human postulated origins of AIDS show how Africa and animals have been constructed as sites of disease: a hypothesis that is problematic. (Rushing, 1995) The mythography of the epidemic is insightful in understanding how western cultural projections reinsert old and perhaps outdated borders between communities and nations that are racial, sexist, homophobic, to sustain a problematic sense of communal immunity under the threat of an epidemic.

Through these accounts communities have attempted to isolate and separate "high risk" individuals, to reinstate as valid traditional biases. The establishment of marginal members as the cause of disease is to ignore how disease is not just a problem of the misfortunate, and how it is always socially constructed. AIDS, for example, has been able to permeate mainstream communities since it cannot be diagnosed early and has a large incubation period, since it can be transmitted through intimate contact with body fluids, and since persons that are HIV+ may not know about it. AIDS has exposed the methods of scapegoating, isolating, and coercion in the dynamic between mainstream communities and peripheral ones, between communities and "high risk" individual members. AIDS has also illustrated how the goals of patients and doctors differ. Patients desire access to any drug that might offer assurance for continual survival and doctors wish to produce scientific (i.e., replicable and standardized) data. (Treichler, 1993)

The AIDS patient can be constructed as informed and resistant to scientific methodologies, willing to subvert standard medical practice to benefit as much as possible from medical technics. The cyborgian situation is similar. We are called to construct a resistant, yet open position from which to examine, and interrogate medico-political knowledges and technologies, so we can learn to be critical and be patients. The challenge of cyborgs is to learn about the costs of living and termination that certain AIDS patients are dealing with through the renewal of funeral ceremonies. Indeed, the problem of cybernetic identity is to face termination as HIV+ persons do from the moment of diagnosis if not before. The question remains how can we construct partial and collaborative identifications that can help us face the limitations and failures of our virtual systems? Clearly we have become fragmented by conflicting wills to power and expertise: will such fragmentation result in more resistant or tacit patients? will we be able though criticism to maintain the object/ subject divisions of these fragmented and fragmenting wills to power and expertise in an un-stabilized fashion that is always emergent and never entirely determined via a fixed imaginary, symptomatic, or real other?

3. What Happens When Cyborgs Are HIV+?: Identities And Resistance

> *For the inherent fear of AIDS is the fear of the polluting touch, the sexualized touch, the touching of polluted products of the body as much as it is a fear of sexual of blood-borne transmission of the disease. And it is a sense of touch associated with race. (Gilman, 216)*

AIDS has tested the boundaries and tolerance of communities and institutions that are racially, sexually, and normatively constructed. AIDS can be viewed as the space where cyborgian creatures are tested against the limits of their own immunity and community, a kind of paradoxical test drive conceived as an accelerating towards the bound of death in this regard immortality would be perfect deceleration, or conversely as a deceleration to the point where the escape form the gravity field of death is impossible and thus immortality would be that very accelerated escape: a kind of rat-race, where the choice would always seem to be towards the pole of immortality. And it is clear how that desire for immortality drives the field of reproduction, sexuality, and even our responses towards death or should I say termination. The question is how to construct identities of resistance that are not riddled by oppositional posturing and polemical gestures, how to invent the act in the age of simulation.

Information and identity interface in the construction of communities and safety or immunity from social ills/ diseases. Are we willing to sacrifice "freedoms" for that sense of communal safety or immunity and to give up the very notion of the individual for an interlaced fabric of identities? Or is freedom, agency, individuality as illusive as the *Enlightenment* quest for liberation that has secured the relation of bodies/ individuals/ communities through scientific and medical knowledge? Can an informatics be separated from strategies of domination between communities and individuals, and would it substantially alter the continuities and discontinuities of the genealogical/ archeological narratives? Are these narratives bound to be as problematic as the current constructions of body, illness, death, and the stories that have linked them?

Medical practice and knowledge have delimited distinct identities: initially by the enclosure of sick and poor individuals in clinics, and then by the rationing of medicine according to income. A current example of how medical technologies construct individuality is fetal surgery that makes the fetus into a patient (that is the closest definition to person-hood), and they are marketed to upper middle class individuals that can afford them. (Casper, 1995) The status and identity of the fetus today are clearly negotiated by medical and political institutions. The fetal patient follows the same route to identity as others, who are also formed by medical technics and political necessities. The AIDS patient is such an identity with a short and intriguing history that has problematized the negotiation of private and public through the debate on confidentiality of medical information, along with the necessity to construct transparent public health policies. In the example of AIDS, contested identities and problematic histories inform each other. Thus, the rooting of new in the old can only occur through the historic reflector/ critic that establishes the linkings of the past-present-future under a genealogy of power. Singular narratives have been deemed necessary for stable political and ideological identifications, so that a singular center of power can be maintained against and despite the rest contesting narratives. The questions arise: are stable identities a political necessity and the only possible basis for resistance, activism, or political responsibility? Do cyborgs require such identities or can identity be established as performative role playing and not be singular?

The process of identification is the foundation not only of institutional processes, but also psychological mechanisms that regulate the demands placed upon individuals. Identity, as such, is formed through imaginary projections via primary and secondary narcissism, and the mirror stage. (Lacan, 1991 and 1977) Identity becomes operational only if it is inscribed, named by the symbolic that has tended to be represented by the genealogical structure of patronyms from fathers to sons. Identity is an imaginary construction mediated by the symbolic network to form the individual as a unified, singular self through the *phallic function*, and is therefore always already performative, always a game between the individual and the other that serves as a mirror (the other being an institution, a computer, a partner). Surveillance is introduced to regulate and stabilize singular identifications, and to guard against criminality, infection, and permeability. Institutional control, also, guaranties that each person would be distinguished by markers, so that a distinct boarder of self and others can be maintained through a mediation of private and public domains.

Cyborgic identities are unsettling because the markers of authentic selfhood have become slippery, changeable, interactive. For example, the identities constructed through internet interactions. Authenticity or originality of individuation vanishes in a sea of replicas and the methods of reduplicating or cloning, which challenge the symbolic naming that monitors and distinguishes self from other. In terms of diseased bodies, the immune system separates self and other, and how it fails can be presently mirrored by AIDS. Thus, "cyborgs incarnate two contradictions of masculine identity. First, they combine phallic masculinity and body permeability. Second they contradict the sociobiological constructions of paternity and maternity." (Fuchs, 1995) Cyborgs challenge the very process of incorporation through reproduction not just because they are born on the limit of the physical, on the border of death, but because the event of death becomes irrelevant when authenticity and individuality are not establishable, when the phallic function fails, when the myth of immunity (bodily or communal) fails.

Gender, race, and class have been essential to the myths and histories of disease and to national identifications that supervise citizenship/ immigration status (as shown in the example of sanatorium), and of course in the current production of AIDS narrative histories. In AIDS narratives, the problematic borders between individuals and communities have been blamed for the absence of immunity. Increased risks to HIV infection have been attributed to faulty masculinity: homosexuality; abnormal lifestyle: class; requirement of blood transfusions: illness; immigrants and aliens: race; drug addiction: deviance; all of which can be theoretically minimized through rational risk reduction and assessment that restores control and re-inscribes a masculine impermeable coat of information over the body. Faulty masculinity has permitted the body to be permeated by such a disease. Masculinity seems to be the boarder most guarded by institutions. However, the establishment of a masculine identifier has strategically avoided been placed in specific contingent situations, or to be represented by an individual case. Except of course in the exceptional, such as Rock Hudson, who has "personified wholesome American masculinity"

(Shilts, 1988: 578) and has been found to be, since he died with an AIDS related condition, gay. Is masculinity as it represents infallibility ever possible?

AIDS, thus, has made evident how masculine, white, rich, and normative are illusive categories, and are constructed upon non-existing ideals of wholeness, strength, purity, immunity that are set up to approximate the ideal of godly immortality. AIDS can be viewed as a space where cyborgic identities arise in the sense that immunity collapses, where the body is permeated by diagnostic technologies to assess the levels of infection, and where it is no longer self-regulated or self-protected. Narratives on diseases such as AIDS have tended to efface individual identities since they are formed upon normative notions of history as a genealogy of continuity through social reproduction. AIDS identities, thus, can shapelift because they mirror current social symptoms, and can illumine the forms in which future communities would be shaped. The identities of AIDS patients have embodied the symbolic/ communal mandates to demark and stabilize a contingent personhood as in the case of the fetus. (Fuchs, 1995) AIDS, therefore, can problematize the institutional methods of identification through surveillance especially by the construction of resistant and informed patients.

The production of medical knowledge has historically been supported by racist, sexist, classist, or generally (if such incorporation is possible) normative divisions in society, which allowed the experimentation on marginal member and their enclosure in hospitals, and thus made marginal individual bodies the key specimens of study. In telematic societies, the medical practitioner may be displaced by the use of an expert system, and the body could be released from the clinical enclosure (except I suppose in "unusual" cases on the limits of medical knowledge). Increased information flows problematize current authentication methods and deny the dream of an impenetrable, perfect information base for governmental authority. Nothing is secure and impermeable in cyberspace. There is a continual development of security systems and of course the birth of a criminal identity: the hacker. (Ross, 1992) The continual (re)production of conflicting knowledges, as a result, may prove problematic in sustaining a singular power base (Lyotard, 1991) that has marked the definition of authority in modern societies.

In virtual space, one may conceive of a forum that avoids the totalizing of modern narratives since "the internet seems to encourage the proliferation of stories, local narratives without any totalitarian gestures, and places the senders and the addressees in symmetrical relations." (Poster, 1995) What seems to be lost is the relations of dominance that have crystallized into a phallic (non-permeable, singular, masculine) authority to governments. Bodily identity in virtual/ information societies loses its material basis, its authentification markers that are stabilized only by a governmental monopoly on the processes of identification and reproduction. As a result, the body becomes fragmented and multiple. The "ideal" unified self is a potential humpty-dumpty, awaiting to be reconstructed through imaginary simulations in cyberspace.

The process of cyborgization, as with all technological advances, has the potential to be dictated by a technocratic elite. The development of cyborgs will tend to follow market pressures and economics in the ways it distributes opportunities for transgressing previous "naturalized" bounds. I map how these processes rework distinct identifications through bodily simulations, which are the site where new technologies (of domination and continual surveillance?) can be introduced. Modes of governmentality become increasingly reliant on technologies of cyber-identification and hypersurveillance that will resolve the problem of determination by default of individual and communal identities. Therefore, it is clear that the sovereign model of power/knowledge will not continue in its present form, where the expert is the central agent, and has to be altered. With the implosion of the modern enclosure, power can no longer have a singular site of operation.

II. The Economics Of Medical Technologies Or The Cyborgs Sale Pitch.

The main trouble with cyborgs, of course, is that they are the illegitimate offspring of militarism and patriarchical capitalism, not to mention state socialism. But illegitimate offsprings are often exceedingly unfaithful to their origins. Their fathers, after all, are inessential. (Haraway, 1991: 153)

The search for a unifying noun is profound because the future of power and relations of dominance is hinged upon a continuity and cyborgs seem to be the most viable candidate: multiple, hybrid, postmodern, illusive, immortal, the mark of the new age, the subject of science fiction narratives.... Cyborgs as imaginative objects have enticed our attention because they have an alien quality, because of their hybridic fusions. An analysis of cyborgs would be incomplete if the mythos of cyborgs and the way they bewitch us is not scrutinized, if their very appeal as our evolutionary future is not investigated and their mystique exposed. Cyborgs have become glamorized in our attempts to confront the intense fragmentation of postmodern critique: but are we willing to purchase the product without further checks just to escape our uncertain predicament, just because we have become weary of the deconstruction of western identities, ideologies, political investments? Is the job complete? Or have we become cynical if I am allowed to talk about a collectivity of some sort? In my analysis of the cyborgic myth, I will use the tools of the materialist historian and the postmodern critic to look at how indeed cyborgs have become the idealized candidates for the future of subjectivity. I will also problematize their very privileged position. It is important to understand in what contexts do cyborgs appear and how they re-figure notions of body and thus subjectivity. The medical context of cyborgic appearance may be considered limited but it is structured and exemplifiable: medical cyborgs have already manifested and are not just sci-fi projections. Thus, I feel it is important to understand the driving force (political, economic, medical) behind current cyborgian transmutations while simultaneously being grasped by the future possibilities.

As the bound of medicine shifted from notions of death to innovations in technology, its object can no longer be termed human, transforming to an intermediary partial bio-artifact. Cyborgs, thus, exist as medical products that attempt not only to transgress previous medical limits (death and disease) but also improve function and image. Cyborgs are the most likely candidates of postmodern subjectivities because they have internalized the surveillance imperatives through technological prostheses, because they can have a total disregard towards personal interestness, because they are replicas of symbolic reproductive mandates. However, cyborgs cannot be faithful to the objectives that have shaped them: they can never be homogenous, self-directed entities, and as such cannot be proper objects or subjects. They are found fluctuating in intermediate, fractal space. The way they use language corrupts the medium, softening harsh lines of contrast, making evident the ways in which objective figures emerge, and are always in a state of emergence from the substantive grounds. Cyborgs become hyper-permeable, constantly re-developing, and re-inventing themselves so that the trace that separates them along with the space from where they emerge can be maintained. They are multiply derived, and their lines of decent are not singular. They look at their distant relative (humans) with awe and suspicion because their ancestors made cyborgic existence inevitable through their unconscious actions. Nothing is unconscious for cyborgs. Things are hyper-real though. Their sensory stimuli are enhanced. So the impute needs to be processed extensively. They can choose which perceptual filters are appropriate for each situation, or to have extensive perception which at times is cumbersome. The doctor-patient relation, an archaic mode of interaction, has been altered or has been in the process of being transformation for some time.

Cyborgs mark a shift in the relations of doctors and patients: a shift that is the product of continual development and revolutionary applications. Even though it would be simplistic to establish a break with the past of medical practice, clearly the information dynamic present in this dyad is changing due to information tech. However, technological prosthetics as regulators of bodily performance and disease suggest that a gap between past/ present is forming. Examples of the growing gap produced by medical technologies abound here are just a few frontiers: imaging technologies that makes the diagnostic procedures less intrusive; expert systems that are used to aid (or guide) doctors through diagnoses with astonishing degrees of accuracy, and that can determine what is the most appropriate, to date, type of action required for a certain patient's case history; reproductive technologies that promise the ability to choose characteristics of children, that push the structure of the family to the limit. The accessibility of specialist medical knowledge through the internet points to the fact that computer networks have the potential to restructure the clinic/ hospital as a physical entity, where the interface of medical knowledge and patients is reformed. Internet communities and groups along with online libraries and web pages can offer directly important information to patients that seek new treatments to diseases like AIDS, where information is essential to survival.

The internet alters the asymmetrical information basis upon which the doctor-patient interaction has been structured; thereby, re-constructing medical practice. Before I attempt to see how the advent of the internet (cine med, medical on-line groups) through AIDS information (Journals and web-pages to name a few sources) can reform the transactions between medicine and patients, I describe how the internet has revolutionized communications and distances, how the operations that mark the body through the circuit of subject-object are exposed, how the limits of previous power-infostructures are pressed and transgressed.

1. Floating In Cyberspace:
Up Against The Limits And Ideals Of Medical Practice

Cyborgs are plugged in cyberspace and are not, however, liberated from previously imposed borders of info-power. The price paid for their increased circulation through net reduces them to a state of immobility. The result is a paradoxical kind of freedom, sexuality, interaction that sterilizes the very (im)possibility of cyber-connection through a hyper-discoursification, in language that no longer represents speech, or that no longer refers to (intimate) relations between individuals. Surfing the net, it becomes evident that "the cyborg point of view is always about communication, infection, gender, genre, species, intercourse, information, and semiology." (Haraway, 1995: XIV) Hyper-interactively occurs through the hyperbolic use of discourse to connect, plug in, permeate, and interfuse with information. However, the "freer" circulation of information does not guarantee "authenticated" knowledge, so universities, governments, hospitals (the modern centers of control) are even more necessary and valuable to ensure that there will be checks, that the wild electronic west (or should I say east?) will obey the laws in the name of some cyber-truths or netiquette, that a sense of order will prevail even in the face of radical transformation, even if the power-centers are no longer enclosures or material spaces.

Power/ knowledge does not necessarily disappear in cyberspace, but is reconfigured in certain ways to re-establish particular kinds of asymmetrical relations based on the ability to access current technologies (class determined). Information flows serve as a basis for the developing models of governmentality and subjectivity: only former asymmetrically fixed relations become reversible, performative, simulated, and less secured. Cyborgs reproduce a body infused with technology and information, a body that is the direct site of textual (re) production. So, "the socioepistemic mechanism by which bodies mean is undergoing a deep restructuring in the latter part of the twentieth century, finally fulfilling the furthest extent of isolation of those bodies through which its domination is authorized and secured." (Stone, 1993: 101) Via the process of bodily isolation and cyborgization, authority and government are re-figured as the mediators and constructors of experts and textually informated corporealities.[5] Governments (or rather modes of governing and disciplining: cybernetics) do not disappear; they become even more indispensable: expertise licensed by authority even more scrutinized and specialized. When to be properly informed is essential, it is even more important to know what information counts and why: to be an expert.

---

[5] The production of bodies in cultural discourse can be studied through textual iconography or bodily representations. The text serves as a surface through which contours of the real can be mapped out and understood in the process of symbolic differentiation based upon power-knowledge. By textual bodies, I mean the very discursive surfaces or coats through which bodies are represented, signified and understood in language: how they always are constructed to support a particular informatics and technologies of domination.

The authority of expertise has been granted by powers of government to universities. Expertise, then, constructs textual bodies that support the genealogies that ensure the continuation of current power-holders. Textual (incoded) bodies become the interface between virtual and physical, between governments and subjects, between individuals and communities. They are a surface through which the physical can be understood, modeled, mediated, and where identity as a function is performed. (Butler, 1994) The acceptance and veracity of textual bodies are hinged upon phallic representations that can convince of their validity through self-evident distinctions performed in spectacle fashion. In cyberspace, the individual control, over textual representation of self-image, allows for the continual transformation of identity though discursive performance. Bodily representations become tailor-made and approach textual ego-ideals because essential, singular, substantive bodies are absent in the interactions between netizens and governments, where new virtual markers need to be established. Cyborgs, thus, establish that "postmodern bodies can shapeshift," (Clarke, 1993: 147), that bodies are infused with technology and information, and that identities always elide, stabilizing and essentializing physical referents. Identities become purely imaginary though checked and mediated by perhaps multivalent symbolics.

The net manifests the failure of a singular symbolic law to survey the body real if most transactions occur in cyberspace. The net allows for a slippage between real and virtual, between the physical presence and simulation (Bogard, 1996) in opposition to "traditional ontology" where "the *Universal* [law] guaranties the *Particular* its[singular] identity." (Zizek, 1994a: 146) The problems of identification, authority, and surveillance that telematic societies introduce are founded upon the inability to secure impermeable and stable borders between private/ public, individual/ communal. Thus, identities are bound to proliferate in cyberspace, and it would be difficult for governments to regulate such a place with the present mode of governmentality. The struggle of AIDS patients for privacy has shown how information flows can be used to monitor individual behavior despite the letter of law, and in the advantage of existing interests. Privacy has been socially constructed, maintained, and supported through power and generally in the benefit of power. Thus, privacy can be trespassed in the interest of governments, insurance companies, the media, and privacy laws simply attempt to mediate information flows between individuals and communities to draw balances between checks and freedoms even if the balance is mostly drawn for the gratification of power structures, and hinged upon their continuation, upon the establishment of a certain order. Floating through cyberspace may not, consequently, be as unfettered or secure as it appears at first sight where information is not secure, where the private domain or personal rights are not yet establishable.

Therefore, no-one can guarantee AIDS patients that access information about treatments virtually that they are not vulnerable since every interaction on the net leaves a trail of data that can be used to infer the status of particular user identities, which may not always reflect persons. Nevertheless, the amount of information on the net is daunting so that such a task is very difficult to say the least. It simply elucidates how surveillance relates to power/ knowledge, how been exempt from extensive surveillance (a private space, a room of one's own) is presently a privilege and not a right. The government through law constructs privacy to "protect" and identify individuals. So it is understandable why "the politics of the body in telematic orders is often articulated around the intersection of medical practice and legal discourse of privacy." (Bogard, 1995:143) Privacy is key to understand how identity becomes localized, secured in the body, how individuals become separated from communities in which they live, guarded through the acts of law that observes, maintains, and constructs the boundary between public/ private. For at least "good" citizens, the law punishes the transgressors of the private/ public boundary, but also retains the right to pry into the private whenever deemed necessary, so that criminality can be exposed and continually checked in the interest of communities. The "punishment" of criminals is the absence of personal rights and privacy: they are under continual surveillance in the prison-panopticon. (Foucault, 1979)

Identity, in telematic societies, loses the direct authentification of *Universal* government, its masculine, impermeable, phallic character, and its substantive, visible markers. Identity becomes inessential, effeminized (Zizek, 1994a) in the sense that it does not exist in direct correspondence or reference to a particular and determinable subject: it is associated with the simulation (non essence) of the real, with performativity. Identity "exists only as the possibility of mediation, transaction, transition, transference" (Irigaray, 1985: 193) between individuals and net-communities; it loses its continual, traditional roots in the blood line (substance) that granted social status and maintained the genealogy of the phallus, thus surrendering the necessity for the name of the father. Privacy laws have promised surety, social order, and stability at the price of surveillance, and stable personal identities or identification mechanisms. Privacy has also historically impinged the free circulation of certain individuals based on their gender, race, class, age, sexuality, employment, state of health, criminality, and so forth. In postmodern societies, the borders of private and public have been continually re-negotiated in terms of the ways these very categories are mediated, in terms of how these identities are conferred.

Governments, libraries, universities, political groups, and parents are evident forces in the negotiating of private/ public in cyberspace: the notable example being the status of "pornographic" materials on the internet, where it can be accessed by persons under age. Hyper-control in post-human, cybernetic, or telematic societies needs to be rethought not through a continually re-established and transgressed division of private/ public that regulates information flows through personal acts, that maintains knowledge in physical enclosures where expertise can only be purchased, but through permeable borders of transparency and confidentiality, through power sharing structures, through the realization of the public's desire to know how and why important decisions are reached. The secrecy over policy making has made such efforts difficult, and only accessible to persons that have a certain degree of education and position.

Policy making (legal and medical decisions) has been constructed upon the secured relations of communities and individuals, governments and citizens, doctors and patients, inside and out, private and public: through the maintenance of property, identity, individuality, agency, responsibility. Information flows are not random; they follow a hierarchy of power that determines the making of systems, where reliability can be pinned on individual decisions and agency. Moreover, data, information, and knowledge differ based upon the degrees of freedom to circulate, to flow, to intermingle, and to be re-interpreted, from raw and un-mediated to highly systemic and organized. However, constructions of individuality and agency have been deemed problematic and chaotic when the information flow does not follow a hierarchical path. An example of the problematic conception of individuality and agency in terms of health is located in the construction of the AIDS patient not as a sufferer of a disease but as the source and agent that caused the disease. (Lewis, 1993)

If information does not follow the path pre-established by the genealogy of power, then "chaos" and "decadence" breaks loose, which represents the fact that responsibility cannot be connected to individual acts or agents, and the results of action become unpredictable, complicated, complex, chaotic, influenced by many factors, multivalent, and can potentially represent catastrophes for the power/ knowledge that needs to interpret, contain, and control them. In extreme circumstances, the catastrophe has been presented by ideological polemics as "godly punishment" as in the case of AIDS. These moments, when the system "heats up," determine the points when new structures of information flows are emerging, whether the flow is determined by economics, ideologies, sexualities. Consequently, increased information flows tend to result in increased entropy, (Hayles, 1995) and the break down of traditional systems of agency, identity, and reliability. "Decadence [then has] threatened in two interconnected ways, both related to energy limited, productive systems -- one artificial, one organic" (Haraway, 1989b: 55) or through the breakdown of the barriers between production and reproduction, where the organic and the mechanical fuse and are undifferentiated, and the body is no longer self-regulating, determined, or a closed system. (Hogle, 1995) Biotechnology has now become necessary to help delimit and regulate the organic system, and medicine provides, develops, designs, and markets such technologies. Nevertheless, the cycle of info-power can not be closed again through technology; it constantly becomes other than what has been: more cyborgic and the state more medicalized.

As a result, "technology plays a major part in consolidating this distancing of the doctor from a necessarily passive patient, leading to the dehumanization of health care" (Wajcman,

1991:71) or put differently, leading to a dehumanizing of the body, which becomes increasingly animal and machine like. Alongside the debate on the dehumanization of health care, the basis for "medical decision making, [which] until very recently, has been a matter of private, not public policy" (Blank, 1988: 233) is changing as the body becomes infused with political, moral, ethical issues. The technologization of medicine has pushed the limits of medical practice as solely a private affair, and has displayed the need for public debate and mediation of biotechnologies through the field of bioethics along with the care, treatment, and information about AIDS patients.

AIDS, as a disease, has contested the barriers between private and public decision making, and thereby attempts to sort out what areas should be primarily confidential (private) or disseminated (public). "Public health care doctors have experienced major difficulties in taking up a collective as opposed to an individualist approach to health needs of the population vis a vis both the rest of the medical profession and government." (Lewis, 1993: 37) However, the need to have flexible and permeable public/ private borders is evident through the mandate of transparency in governmental affairs. Individual (personal) data and information can be construed as property in contrast to solely public matters. The difficulty lies in determining exactly which information is personal and which collective. However, with more information flowing, it will be difficult to secure information that is deemed to be private, making the delineation of proper use and misuse, a code of conduct necessary. Through the troubles that the net poses, it also will become clearer which information should be kept secured and on what grounds if such case would exist. The scenarios have to be contextually determined so that it will become apparent what is ethical and appropriate in which situation, e.g., could super-markets or any such agency that collects data about weekly food consumption be allowed to sale data without individual consent and is such collection constitutional?

Increased information flows can be used to construct knowledgeable and resistant patients (or consumers of biotech) able to make more informed decisions about differing treatments evident in the case of confrontations over therapies for AIDS (although medicine and biotechnology are not solely determined by a disease discourse). AIDS has made clear how classifications construct information barriers, and make knowledge powerful. This circuit of power can be broken down by activism and alternative methods of informing. (Treichler, 1993) Information technologies also contest the hierarchical barriers to info-flows and make increasingly difficult the task of securing information or of balancing confidentiality and right to access data as determined by the example of medical screening. (Towers, 1993) To understand how technologies and ethics need to be integrated into policy making, it is important to construct a participatory or interactive forum that can guide individual choices. Whether the burden of responsibility would be placed on collectivities, on individuals, or if such entities are not any more relevant, depends on the specifics of each case scenario, and should not be solely secured upon one or the other. In a sense we can start imagining the notion of hyper-privacy that integrates intimacy and privacy, presence and absence, closeness and distance, (Bogard, 1996), collectivity and individuality, that can then be defined only in terms of a dynamic balancing of transparency and security of information: defining in detail perhaps for what purposes information acquired can be used and by whom or indeed if not bothering with such distinction is operable. If all is visible, would it be ethical? The latter scenario would require an entirely different frame of governmentality than we have.

The increase of information flows raises questions of legitimacy and surveillance that also re-instate the requirement of control, authority, government. The novel prospects of governmentality are not determined by a solid singular basis of power, by a representative structure, or by closed circuit of narrative genealogies of power, but through an improved participation and feedback in the production of information, knowledge, logos, through a more direct or telematic democracy with increased social responsibility and expertise. It is certain that "We cannot afford the versions of the 'one dimensional man' critique of technological rationality, which is to say, we cannot turn scientific discourses into the Other, and make them into the enemy while still contesting what nature will be for us. We have to engage in those terms of practice, and resist the temptations to remain pure." (Haraway, 1993a: 5) Engagement and contestation are fundamental in the creation and articulation of cyborgic narratives that mark the interaction between technology, medicine, and law: individuals, communities, and government. Through these narratives we can begin to discern the operations of participatory agency and note the contours of the hyper-subject, cyber-patient, and netizen.

2. Participation, Feedback, & Infostructure: The Stories of Cyborgic Creations

> The replacement of the natural body by the artificial body of the organization entails a transformation in the production as well as politics of reproduction. That is, the technologies for the making of men devised in naturalist discourse provide an anti-naturalist and anti-biological alternative to biological production: the mother and the machine are, in the naturalist text, linked but rival principles of creation. (Seltzer, 1992: 157)

Simulation technology has destabilized the connection of identity to bodily markers (even genetic fingerprinting, which has been the last "real" mark, has also become problematic with the advent of cloning). Similarly, deconstruction has displaced the link of the system signifier/ signified to the naturalistic referent, (the linguistic articulation of the connection between signifier, signified, referent is the basis of Saussurian structuralism), (Saussure, 1974) and has illustrated how meaning is deferred through an interconnected network of play and signification, of de-centered centeredness. (Derrida, 1978a) The distinctions between suppression and simulation are key to understanding how the structure of language and meanings alters in hyperreal societies. Traditionally, the (real) thing is simply suppressed in the transaction between subjects. The network of meaning of "the symbolically structured universe we live in [has been] organized around a void, an impossibility (the inaccessibility of the Thing itself)." (Zizek, 1992:181) Simulation evades and exposes the suppression of the thing through hyperbolic representation, but it doesn't guarantee direct access to the thing, rather it reconstructs the thing in interactive space: where the contours of the real in discourse can be continually contested and changed, as a result the thing is re-invented in cyberspace.

The concept of interactivity presupposes participation and feedback of users and players. Since the subject loses its substantive basis, it can only be constituted by the moves produced in the game of simulation, structured by the user-computer interface, by the abilities of each player to program new options or to transgress the given rules. Through the net, the subject can only be partially identified and determined, and thus is more capable of transgression. The identity of the hacker, who is a central in the understanding of postmodern gaming and criminality, rises as a result. In the computer criminal scene, the trespasser tends to be of an upper middle class background reversing the stereotypical situation of a lower class deviant (Ross, 1991) which simply says something about the class status of the computer medium. However, hackers have been glorified as well as condemned to large fines. The main difficulty is that it is hard to identify by who and how a system has been broken into, and plenty of cyber-trespasses go unnoticed. Hackers constantly develop strategies to invade security systems and these systems continually change as a result. The revolution of computers has brought about other vices as well such as viruses, worms, or trojans that infect/ invade systems, and destroy data, computer files, or even hardware. One can see a whole semiotic field of forms developing through these transgressions and their curtailment.

The relation between the simulation of codes and language (as the primary code of inscription) may become more evident. Simulation can be conceived as a third order appearance, where the code is not just linguistic, where it becomes self-generative and transforming, where it forgoes the representation of things as secured upon a stable word- image connection, where it transcends the mapping into a discursive code in which the slippage between words, images, and things is inevitable (second order). (Baudrillard, 1983) The most elementary form of representation has been conceived in the pre-Babylonian one to one correspondence of word-images and things, the long lost dream of a natural language (first order). (Baudrillard, 1983) Computers have facilitated the "replacing [of] linguistic signs with circuit arrangements and cerebral operations with electronic play of these circuits." (Goux, 1990: 129) Thus the symbolic, regulative domains of discourse, language, information become increasingly computer dependent, virtualized, hyper-textual, becoming de-contextualized and liquid.

"The modern computer represents a new breakthrough in inscription: an operational writing that manipulates mindless, desemantised signs." (Goux, 1990: 129-130)

Simulation implies an end to the primacy of language over other codes of interconnection. The resulted hyper- interactivity of the system computer-user with other players shows that the connections of agency-individuality-identity have to be refigured to match the emergent computer interface between institutions and persons, and have to be restructured through a model of participation and intercourse that can only confer a variable and varying structure, for meaning, signification, individuation. The change that simulation implies to the code does not entail, however, the end of discipline and surveillance. The encapsulation of things in the code through word-images has been only possible through observation, confinement, and discipline. (Foucault, 1979) With the emergence of simulation as third order appearance, the implication is that novel forms of control, of hypersurveillance have to be mapped. (Bogard, 1996)

Clearly different modes of power/ knowledge would result from differing modes of supervision, and the key for the future of power-sharing will be to participate and re-negotiate the relation of private-public, individual-collective, self-other. Participation (in politics, education) has been mediated by the private/ public boarder. Education is essential in constructing expertise, and thus the privilege of active participation in public affairs. Evidently access to literacy and knowledge has been constructed on the grounds of class, race, gender, sexuality, age, citizenship status.... The privileged access to education has granted elites the ability to formulate discourses and contain ones that do not have access to education (or the methods of systematizing information into knowledge). Problematizing the bounds between lay and elite have been recent: this distinction been the last constitutive marker of class in technocratic societies. As mirrored on such a distinction one can understand the success of western medicine and science, which is hinged upon the domination and marginalization of non-western (or alternative western) practices and knowledges. (Harding, 1993)

The violation of pre-established bounds of race, class, gender in the transactions of knowledge constitutes an act of resistance that can be facilitated by the postmodern breakdown of information barriers and distances. The ability to participate in the directing/ dictating of the future is based upon the availability of the tools and methods that organize information into knowledge (in marxist terms the tools of (re)production not just of things but info-commodities). Scientific and/ or technological illiteracy in an information world undermines the processes of participation, social responsibility, and mobility with the effect of constructing fixed dynamics that lead towards reactionary social determinisms, that construct stabilized technocratic centers of power in the position to direct the future by determining the position of others through class and opportunity. Social determinisms in the absolute take the form of biological fixation especially in the example of the medicalization or biologization of social problems under the Nazi regime,

(Proctor, 1993) or even the construction of socio-biological propositions that present the individual to be dominated by pre-established genetic codes alterable only through genetic engineering or selective breeding (otherwise termed as racial cleansing: eugenics).

The Nazi example displays the dangers of totalitarian (or ultra-masculinist) ideologies that are impermeable by Others, that attempt to construct pure bounds with regard to race or any such category for that matter. Telematic societies can become problematic if hyper-surveillance reaches the panopticon ideal of total control as materialized in Orwell's novel *1984*. When social operations become completely virtualized, they can allow for increased participation through the availability of information, and the modes of information processing into knowledge. Then, technological and scientific processes will become more accessible, and the contours of the future as established upon knowledges will not fall into the trap of totalitarian absolutism. Telematic societies can furbish a new model of power based upon a transparency in the interactions between individuals and communities, and a public participation in government, policy making, expertise through cyberspace. Thus, power would not have a singular center, but it would be determined through a governmentality permeable by social participation, and not fixated on perfect boundary control even if the power-holders change periodically. When power sharing would not be an oxymoron, then agency would be purely performative and didactic.

To understand agency as a transgression of boundaries means to see how the systems of community/ identity/ individuality, of government/ citizen/ alien, of medicine/ patient/ sick body, become inter-permeated, their boundaries fuzzy. The act as transgression "means to assume the risk that what I am about to do will be inscribed into a framework whose contours elude my grasp, that it may set in motion an unforseeable train of events, that it will acquire a meaning different from or totally opposed to what I intended to accomplish -- in short, it means to assume one's role in the game of 'cunning reason.'" (Zizek, 1994b: 31) To assume the responsibility of one's role not only to play and participate in the game of government, but to engage and contest the rules of governmental procedures, of standard power relations is essential to allow for the underprivileged members of communities to acquire the skills and abilities required for information assessment, decision making so that current info-structure barriers can be transgressed and alternative narrative histories, knowledges, genealogies constructed. History, as a narrative genealogy, should not be reduced to the function of justification or call for action (Nietzsche, 1980), rather histories are key in the (re)production and enrichment of culture in the postmodern sense, so that a coexistence or symbiosis of old and radically new can be conceived in the mirror of time, turned upon itself to allow for various assortments.

In the case of AIDS, the agency and responsibility for the epidemic proportions of the disease has fallen upon individual sufferers, not policy makers who could have contained the number of cases had they allowed for and acknowledged the need of persons engaged in "risky" activities to be informed, and had they presented that information in a non-judgmental fashion. A direct example is the conflicts over to control of HIV infection as transmuted by infected needles and the surrounding controversy about encouraging drug use and deviant behavior. (Anderson, 1993) A similarly problematic preposition of the US congress: the *Immigration Act*[6] has been to limit the immigration status of HIV+ persons even if such limitations do not apply to other diseases such as influenza or tuberculosis, and to deny treatment to such persons even if their immigration status has been legally approved. Issues of morality (i.e., the encouragement of deviant behavior) collide with the needs for ***public*** medical policy to curtail infection in a ***non-discriminating fashion***. These normative and traditional arguments have presented information about HIV transmission, about safer practices through the use of condoms or clean needles as infectious to the social body, as a promotion of the very "deviant" activity that "induced" the disease. Such arguments collapse the distance between information and infection, knowledge and immunity, morality and health policies, while constructing the risky activity as the cause of disease, and thus the sufferer as worthy of the infection.

Agency, causality, responsibility are re-constructed in telematic societies through the active contestation of the rules that form the game of interaction, sexuality, desire. The current debates over legality and illegality of information or user activities in cyberspace cannot be underlined enough since they potentially shape the format of future interactions between users and institutions, and they will also constitute the contours that the game of identity and surveillance take in cyberspace. Most transactions will become hyperreal since such connections diminish distances and allow individuals to be at different places simultaneously while simultaneously minimizing the operational costs for businesses and governments. With the cheapening of the technologies necessary for cyber-action, transactions in cyberspace will be more economically viable and encouragingly less class determined. We can begin to imagine the electronic mall, agency, university, hospital. Such institutions would be more regulatable and standardized. The doctor (as practitioner), the salesclerk, the representative could be displaced by the expert system as the database that interfaces users with more or less reliable information.

Since all or at least most interactions will become hyperreal in telematic societies, the surveillance of hyper-bodies becomes paramount in cyberspace, but also in real-space where security systems have introduced short circuit television, monitoring streets, stores, highways of

---

[6] The US Immigration Act was signed to law before the US elections in November 1996. Some of the effects of this law can be seen in *Independent* newspaper article, page 17, April 4 1997: "Panic Among Immigrants Over US Law."

course excluding the homes of "good" citizens to date that define the last refuge of "privacy." The home as a refuge of privacy is already permeated by the internet, telephone, television, mail, and its boundaries are challenged along with the independence, individuality of self/ body. The stories of disembodiment and loss of self abound since they mark the end of modern conceptions of self, home, as a loss of innocence represented in horror/ slasher films. On the other hand, cyborgic accounts remain in a state of emergence and have a futuristic quality to them. They attest to being hybrids of human/ animal/ machine, and to establish transient identities through an amalgamation that joins strategies of domination and resistance, of information and knowledge, of substance and essence, in a dynamic contestable symbiosis. The narrative as a historical model has constructed agents and encounters, whereas cyborgic creation stories highlight transformation as key to the permeation and confrontation of the contours that establish cyber-identity.

A cyber-account is created by a infusion with history not as a progression but a dromology towards alterity, constantly excavating texts and knowledges that re-establish other points of reference, that reconfigure techno-organic relations. Cyborgs are engaged in medical practice and policy that is no longer of necessity private. Furthermore, they cannot remain part of a secured private domain in hyperreal affairs that are in the present setting solely public. Medicine is, thus, called to construct public accounts of textual bodies that can sustain social (re)production (even through cloning), that can preserve a sense of governmental order in the face of death, disease, accident, or radical transformation. Bodies in the new schema of things are fragmented, yet they retain at times "'the system of differences' that attributes differential value to different bodies according to traditional, dualistic 'natures.'" (Balsamo, 1996: 159) However, even in the attribution of values and differences to bodies, hyper-codes produce only partial identifications, which seem to be the only possibility in the relations between fragmented bodies and multifaceted institutions. The encounters between cyborgs via the net are structured by fluid architectures that mirror the contested, but always negotiating and facilitating centers of power that generate these partial identifications.

3. Bodily Encounters:
The Permeability Of Self And The Instability of Identity

> A certain fragility has been discovered in the very bedrock of existence -- even, and perhaps above all, in those aspects of it that are the most familiar, most solid and most intimately related to our bodies and to our everyday behavior. But together with this sense of instability and this amazing efficacy of discontinuous, particular, and local criticism, one in fact also discovers something that perhaps was not initially foreseen, something one might describes precisely the inhibiting effect of global, totalitarian theories. (Foucault, 1995: 19-20)

Attempting to generate genealogical accounts that critic bodily encounters with others (human, animal, mechanical, textual, institutional, cyborgic) is problematic if we purge the text from the constitutive processes of virtualization and simulation. As a result, it is key to move beyond the need for subjectification or objectification to a discourse of interaction and partial determination. A critique of self-referentiality is not enough to understand the formulation of human sciences and the practices of power if strategies of domination have been conceived at the very basis of discourse. (Habermas, 1995) With the re-invention of surveillance in telematic orders, one has to re-situate the relation of subject, object, to delineate how hyper-discoursification affects the linguistic code as it has been founded upon the distinction between artifact and organism/ human and animal.

In the continual chatter of cyber-interaction, we are forced to confront and mirror ourselves with the computer, with radical alterity, and with others trapped in the game of co-determination and symbiosis, trapped in the network of signification and identification. "'We,' in these discursive worlds, have no routs to connection other than through the radical dismembering and dis-placing of our names and our bodies. We have no choice but to move through a harrowed and harrowing artifactualism to elsewhere." (Haraway, 1993b: 25) The move to elsewhere is possible through the continual transgression and contestation of our identity to meet the other and choreograph an erotic dance of mystic and information, of action and gesture, of truth and falsehood beyond the threat of aphanisis and groundlessness. To be cyborgic is then to be radically permeable, unstable, and changeable, not secured through self-referents: *I*. "Alterity [then] is the very possibility and process of embodiment: it conditions but is also a product of the pliability or plasticity of bodies which makes them other than themselves, other than their 'nature,' their functions and identities." (Grosz, 1994: 209)

Bodily markers of gender, race, disease lose their constitutive material character in the interactions between institutions and individuals in cyberspace. However, other markers that relate to user status as belonging to an expert elite, as belonging to a specific class or background can be determined, but these determinations will always run the risk of being trespassed. Thus, such user-identities could not be deemed as reliable, fixed, or secure. As a result, secured-singular power basis cannot be stabilized on identity as ground. It would alleviate some of the growing friction between meticulously stratified groups in the interest of current power-holders if methods of being inclusive are developed, so that conflicts with regard to the hold of power can be avoided. Inclusivity would be key to power-sharing and symbiotic governing architectures that would not efface diversity, that would rather displace *phallic **difference***. *Difference* (as mirrored by the separation of powerful/ powerless) is a method through which power can be retained by genealogies of dominance. I am not talking about the present talk about the plurality of differences, but rather about the primary opposition, about the ***a-priori difference*** between *Universal* and *Particular* as articulated by Hegel, a kind of axiomatic ***Difference***.

The *Difference* par-excellence is the constitutive fiction that establishes it-self in conflict with the Other as a assemblage of others, and in supposed interest of the Other. However, it has been clear that dialectics establish the Difference that is always already presuppose in a circularly closed fashion. To escape such circuit of power-determination, governments should be required to maintain an all inclusive forum as the principal site of decision making that negotiates the encounters between netizens and institutions. Direct participation would thereby require a flexible, fluid format of power that is shared between many interdependent centers of responsibility, who are not concerned with a fixation of a power dipole as established presently by majority determination. The maintenance of an interactive, collective, collaborative enclosure that is archetectured to allow multiplicity and diversity to remain is important to warrant the underrepresented to influence policies that affect them. The study of governmentality would then be the study and construction of structures of participation and activism in the context of political and epistemological decision making. In the case of AIDS, the interactions, between officials and patients/ activists, have been structured upon the traditional dynamic of powerful/ powerless, a structuring that has produced the delayed reaction to the epidemic. One still discerns: "almost no increased effort to meet the needs of the poorest, the most vulnerable, the most isolated, or the least powerful." (Mann, 1992: 788)

Permeable borders between information centers and the uninformed equalize the dipole of power, and allow for a different basis of participation that can materialize in cyberspace. Health policy makers need to determine a public agenda beyond basic research and therapy, to establish a format/ forum of social interaction and information permeation of traditionally held borders. Increased info-flow in this fashion would allow people in disadvantaged positions to benefit from the knowledge about the epidemic, to transgress their predetermined social situation: "vulnerability to HIV infection and its impact decrease where public health principles and human rights are respected." (Mann, 1992: 786) AIDS has prompted the construction of discourses that regulate the intimate encounters of bodies, that mediate the encounters of self and other. Risky identities, thus, have been stabilized in the interaction between individuals and institutions that can sustain or supplant resistant collective identifications. Interestingly, claims to self-determination (through resistance) always have the structure of fiction in contrast to symbolic mandates that present their grasp of power in the garments of truth. Discursive determinations of sexuality that is defined as the intimate interaction between self and others are key to the economics of AIDS identifications. The regulation of desire through discourse of sin and disease has established as Universal the normative mode for fulfillment of material and personal needs, for the determination of status and the materialization of happiness in exclusion to practices that have been deemed excessive or without any "productive" or "reproductive" function. This regulation of desire is possible only through a confessional setting whether priestly, psychiatric, or interpersonal, where one can be redeemed and included into the 'book of life,' i.e., normative history and family genealogy.

This regulation of desire is not possible without singular identifications. So when the hold of governmental institutions on the verification or verifiability of identity is not absolute and identity can be destabilized, then signifiers that secure the control of identity upon material markers such as colour, sexual organs, attire, property, behavior, and so forth would be undermined. Making "explicit the silencing, submersion, and containment of [more than] half of humanity effected in the most 'rational', 'civilized' and 'noble' of cultural activities, the violence of coercion veiled beneath the most glorified and pure of 'human endeavors' -- the creation of knowledges." (Grosz, 1989: 230) What is at stake is not knowledge itself, but the current structure of power/ knowledge, the prevailing form of governmentality and certainty generation, the present "social fabric" as formulated through the mediation of interactions between individuals, in other words the unwritten social contract. I guess feminisms can be envisioned as the discursive practices that attempt to construct permeable borders, collaborative identifications, coalitional politics, that can determine new modes of participation, activism, and subversion of traditionally secured power structures. Feminist undertakings attempt to expose the fact that "knowledge is produced not only within a socioeconomic and political framework, but also an intellectual tradition with stated and un-stated assumptions." (Lazreg, 1990: 327)

Feminisms have painfully confronted their own boundary assumptions about the "essence" of woman and have opened up to contestations of women of colour, differing sexual orientations, class status, and alternative modes of knowledge production. Feminism as an umbrella term is highly contested and multivalent. Identifications need to be similarly contested and conflicting to remain un-stabilized and to resist being inscribed into a teleological genealogy, a singular, historical narrative, an a priori universal difference, an absolute truth. In so far as history is viewed within perspective not as factual, then power as derived from narrative knowledges and histories can be constantly kept in check. Freedom, then, could be this moving beyond a self-contended knowledge of the elusiveness of independence, action, identity (Hegel, 1953) to the importance of re-establishing the game of signification, of co-determination, and of contestation through inclusion and not an essentializing *Difference*.

Medicine, as any knowledge system, is faced with the challenge to reconfigure its objectives in the face of postmodern critiques, to facilitate an openness (freedom?) and participation in the construction of expertise. Cyborgs contest present medical objectives to allow for a more open-ended movement of knowledge as information. They require a shift from the medical desire to invent cures for new diseases or variants (while codifying, containing, controlling the body), to designing prosthetics for post-humans so that they can transgress their (immunological) limits in the face of disease or new and unfamiliar terrains. I examine the forces at play in this shift of medical objectives: examining in whose interests present changes occur, how cybernetics can bring together human and natural sciences, and what impact does this contact have on the way medical knowledge is structured and disseminated. The role of medicine in determining state policy on public health needs to be rethought along with the rest of the social info-structure. It is certain that medical knowledge and practice change as a result of technological innovation. The questions are: in which direction will medicine transform? what factors are important in both checking and implementing the most beneficial transformations?

Economically, the postindustrial landscape demonstrates that the demand on (post)human capital for industrial production has decreased; the notion of a factory as the site of commodity manufacture has been imploded, becoming increasingly specialized in the production of parts. Thus, technological innovations and the service industry have become the motivating forces of economic growth. The means of production are less human labour dependent and increasingly technologically driven. In the expert-knowledge industry, the technological frontier can be formulated in terms of an intelligent cybernetic preceptor that would allow for the displacing of humans as the mediators and builders of knowledge. One can envisage cyborgs with enhanced memory, computation, and perception functions to occupy such a place. At present we would have to strain our imagination to see how medicine can operate without doctors, politics without politicians, universities without teachers, how the challenge would be in the designing of new technologies of power sharing (I trust) through contestation and inclusivity. As such an undertaking, I will examine how cyborgs become the third millennium medical products, and how they can be constructed as the participators/ contestors of the game of knowledge, expertise, technology, and governmentality, by showing how the medical game can be altered through cybernetic innovations.

III. Cyborgs As The Third Millennium Medical Projects

> For postmodern approaches, class is clearly and commonly involved for the "new" reproductive technologies are mostly very expensive, usually uncovered by private or state plans, and also very unevenly distributed. (Clarke, 1995: 149)

Medical practices have been clearly impacted by technological innovations throughout historical development. Technology has altered the way medicine has conceived of bodies, diseases, and death. The list is expanded to include borders of production/ reproduction, human/ animal/ artifact: the sites where cyborgs are born. Some questions arise: what degrees of livability are produced in the postmodern medical scene? should medical technologies (reproductive or otherwise) be class determined? and could medical policies transgress the limits imposed by class to allow extensive public access? The shifting of medical objectives is codetermined by changes in individual/communal notions of identity, agency, individuality. Consequently, "agency should not be seen as a twofold, individual and societal, phenomenon, but as a multilevel one, where individual and societal levels are integrated because of the special make up of the agents -- their social characterization. It is this level of sociality that throws a bridge between individual and collective action." (Gilbert & Count, 1995: 8) This level of sociality allows for a re-conceptualization of identity as resistance and activism (if the act is to be constructed as a transgression of pre-determined info-boarders) while destabilizing the notion of resistance in contention of a Universal standard. Resistance can be conceived in terms of a critical stance that is always emergent, where the center is never occupied by any specific group that can claim normative or Universal status. Cyborgic identities are resistant in their hybridic composition.

Cyborgs can be conceived as the next millennium medical products because they are the outcome of the restructuring in political, social, and medical spheres as altered by technological innovation. In conceiving sociality, governmentality, cybernetics, one can locate the impetus underlying most of the present postmodern deconstructions or critiques. A re-conceptualization of the connection between information and knowledge as structured by power dipoles has been key to these critiques. Cyborgs, thus, are symptomatic of these altering conditions in the state of info-power, and therefore have the quality of mythos: they appeal to imaginary sci-fi projections. Yet in these times it has become evident that "the boundary between science fiction and social reality is an optical illusion." (Haraway, 1991: 149) I illustrate through the example of the patient/ doctor info-power dipole how technology has the potential to alter the unequal ground of information, and can enable the use of the tools for information processing, making, thus, fixed power-dynamics obsolete. However, if info-power has become less localized, it does not necessarily imply an emancipation or liberation that is why the cyborgic identity needs to be constructed upon a resistance, in a perpetual state of emergence, rather than a re-found fixity.

The body as a discursive-material entity has been constructed as the site of subjectivity, as the locus of inter-fusion between communal and individual. The medical body has given way to cyborgic transmutation, which calls into question fixed notions of individuality, responsibility, and agency as they have been stabilized upon supposed material and unalterable contours. Agency as a conception that is founded upon concretized bodies has been challenged since traditional/ corporate structures of linear reliability and responsibility are contested along with the "traditional equation of 'labour + raw materials = economic success.'" (Barrett and Pruitt, 1994: 383) One can discern a concretized formulation of an informatics of domination as it has been established upon the identity of an emergent technocratic elite: the ones who hold the latest technologies. Nevertheless, their grasp of the means of technological innovation is gradually contested especially since it cannot assert itself in the benefit of only a particular group.

The site of techno-info-power (though continually contested and contesting) is the cyborg as techobody, as conceived though the meeting of natural and human sciences in the construction of cybernetic systems that can potentially manufacture intelligent bio-artifacts, whose precursors are computerized systems. Technology has been projected as the answer to many problems: it provides solutions and treatments to disease and diagnosis; it promises the securing (of credit-card) identity (through digital microchip implants) even if it radically contests the border between human/ natural/ artificial; it produces the opportunity for increased participatory democracies: where the nation will no longer be the sole-holder of power; it suggests the possibility of the global village where time/ space collapse, where distance does not matter. It almost sounds like a telecom commercial that links the present to the future and sells the stocks that matter at very low prices. And it sounds too good to be true especially when global wealth is unevenly distributed between a handful of individuals who happen to be the holders of emergent computer-technologies, e.g., Bill Gates and the like. And of course the costs of technologization are under-rated as we leap to meet the future.

The notion of power is established upon asymmetrical relations, upon an uneven distribution of wealth, opportunity, information, knowledge. As the traditional notions of success become less relevant in the information world, it will be even more essential to understand how the transformation of asymmetrical relations de-center the concept of power from a *Particular/ Universal*, a visible seat or throne, to reproduce an intricate network of control and resistance as understood through governmentality: the establishment and authorization of expert systems. Cybernetics can be seen as the expertise that has provided the basis for contemporary telematic societies (the computer) that of course does not measure up to the promised robot (servant or master?) although the field of robotics is in boom especially in Japan. My main concern is it to ask how and if technology can become less class determined. However, the function of the global/local state can provide ways to permeate class borders through educational opportunities, to allow for diverse backgrounds to access the skills necessary to survive in an information world. This would be the main purpose for the state's existence.

1. Cybernetics: The Meeting Of Natural and Human Sciences

> Up to now the machines built and used by man have worked almost exclusively on the material plane. We have built machines that could do things far beyond the physical force of man. We have built machines that allowed us to conquer space and time to make matter and energy work for us. We have invented machines that calculate faster than man and that have a more retentive memory. What we have not done is to create machines more 'intelligent' than man, for the electronic brains we create are our servants not our masters. (Boulanger, 1969: 8)

Cybernetics is the field that attempts to integrate behavioral, biological, and technological expertise, and is "the art and science of government." (Clark, 1969: 109) In other words, "it is the basic science underlying the process of homeostasis in biological systems and automation in industry, and its implications are being applied in economic and social planning." (Porter, A., 1969: vii) Cybernetics has not acquired a concrete academic status to date principally because it requires an interdisciplinary approach. Its applications can be seen in the field of biotechnology and some social science uses manifest under the guise of science and technology studies/ cyberology. What has characterized the development of cybernetics is the establishment of control and feedback operations that work on various types of systems, that can distinguish machines from automatons (if human energy is not expended in operating it then it is considered fully mechanized). (Demczynski, 1969) Cybernetic are those devices that "employ the principles of feedback or digital computation or both extensively." (Demczynski, 1969: 23)

The cybernetic challenge has been to construct a device that is not dependent upon clear human instructions and programming, that can perceive and codify data not just process whatever is imputed, that is able to self optimize, goal-seek, and learn. Consequently, info-power in cybernetic societies can then be understood by the ability "to increase our mental capabilities" (Demczynski, 1969:27) through technological prosthetics. In taking up the cybernetic challenge, one produces hazy borders between living and artifact, human and machine. These hazy boarders imply that such ontologies may no longer be relevant, that they have been always problematic or simplistic, and that they need to be reconstituted not however in terms of primary oppositions that draw sharp contrasts. I establish how the distinction between living and artifact is no longer relevant by primarily focusing on the interface of cybernetics/ biotechnologies with biological, behavioral, and medical systems, to determine how cybernetics has revolutionized information processing and communications, how indeed the resulting info-structures can become the basis for the future of power-sharing.

In the example of medicine, the form of general practice can be summarized by the *Table 1.1*. It can be divided into three stages: history, diagnosis, treatment. The power-dynamic (dipole) of doctor/ patient can be mirrored by the pupil/ teacher relation. (Clark, 1969: 131) As shown, the doctor/ patient relationship has been represented by the teacher/ pupil power-dynamic with a reversal and a period during diagnosis when there is no dynamic, when medicine as discourse determines the strategy the doctor follows. This portrayal is simplistic but illustrative of the traditional medical info-dipole and the process that governs the distribution of treatment. Uneven information distribution and differential skills in processing it to knowledge establish the dynamic between pupil and teacher, and clearly such is the case for doctors and patients although the pupil may have the chance to become a teacher, the patient rarely becomes or is a doctor. *Table 1.1* acknowledges that an informational differential is what causes the dynamic between doctors and patients, yet makes clear that the doctor and patient are both subjected to medical discourse that regulates them and delimits the possibilities for treatment. In this case scenario the role of medicine, as discourse, had not been substituted by the use of expert systems, so that the control it exerts on doctors tends to have the form of peer review, or other methods of standardization and surveillance.

In constructing cybernetic systems that assist doctors during diagnosis, the level of medicine as database is introduced, where the computer diagnostician as it represents medical knowledge dictates what kind of strategy is required (of course up to date). Presently, it has been up to the doctor to agree or not to consider the options offered by the database (DB) or even to disregard them altogether. In this regard, diagnostic technologies for medicine today operate the same way as the systems that assist pilots in high tech warfare. The "pilot's associate" is a crude example as to how cybernetic tactics are used to supplement human decision making. (DASPA, 1995) Is the human factor indispensable? Will the doctor as a mediator of medical knowledge be disposed by an intelligent systems or should I call them cybernetic (governed) as in the case of self-guided missiles? Of course to consider the development of wetware (that is direct computer/ human linkage through corporeal probes), as in the case of the jet pilot, implies that the status of a sole human operator is under revision. Then, we can no longer clearly differentiate the pilot from the associate and would have to speak of the pilot/ associate system as fully cybernetic. These issues are important to understand how the development of cybernetic preceptors affects the place of experts in increasingly cybernetic societies, along with how the notion of power will be transmuted to become less locally determined, while remaining connected with knowledge and information distribution.

Table 1.1: On the Stages of Medicine.

State of Medicine	The Role Of The Doctor	The Role Of The Patient
1. History, Physical Examination, Special Investigation	Pupil	Teacher
2. Diagnosis	——	——
3. Treatment	Teacher	Pupil

A few points about *Table 1.1*, the relationship between patients and doctors is not as reversible as the table presents. The doctor almost never plays the pupil in the physical examination as the patient never plays the teacher since he/ she does not have direct knowledge of the condition in which their body is if they did they would produce the diagnosis on their own and wouldn't need the doctor to do it for them. In telematic societies when the access to medical knowledge and diagnostic techniques (as in databases or diagnostic programs) by the patient increases, then the prospect of following the treatments prescribed by such diagnostic devices without the presence of a physician to monitor (excluding the exceptional cases where treatment is not standard or has failed) would become commonplace. If the prescribed treatment fails, then perhaps the execution factor would be at fault. If indeed treatment has been followed correctly, then one would need to follow other treatments that are available. As such, the dynamic of patient/ diagnostician becomes more equalized. Diagnostic technologies can eventually become embodied self-regulating prosthetics. In such a case, it is clear that the doctor would no longer have a privileged access to medical knowledge and thus the information dipole could be reversible/ performative, depending simply on upgrades (i.e., CyberMed 2.5).

The advent of specialized user groups or net-pages, where information on AIDS treatment can be accessed, where options about treatment can be disseminated directly to the patient, along with where and by whom the treatment is offered, demonstrates how the information base of doctors and patients has altered with the advent of the internet. One can browse through the options, and link to the online medical library even if sometimes such services are at a relative high cost. The importance of accessibility[7] of such information by patients has been acknowledged by the National Library of Medicine[8] that has presented some

---

[7] There are many web pages on the internet that provide patient information an example is ARIC (AIDS Information Center) which seeks to empower patients through information but also goes through the pains of stating that treatment should only be administered by a physician in case of pending suits. Their address is http://www.critpath.org/aric/.

8 The web page for the National Library of Medicine can be located at: http://www.nlm.nih.gov/

information to organizations such as AEGIS,[9] offering both funds and direct access. Overall, though, the prospect of on-line information tends to be class bound although efforts have been made to reduce the costs of these services. In cyberspace, one can access multimedia takes on the latest medical knowledge in virtual reality form (although such services tend to be commercial).[10] Cyberspace is not the only example where the dynamic of doctor/ patient as established by privileged access to information is challenged.

The development of expert systems as diagnosticians is another emerging site that contests the doctor/ patient dipole especially when it can be placed in public use through cyberspace, which can grant (potentially) free access to many people from different parts of the world as well. Expert systems that incorporate preceptor probes have the potential of replacing the doctor as practitioner. Further, the cybernetic-diagnostician can be considered as a *simulation* of the process of diagnosis that most doctors are trained to do. This simulation is not simply the synthesis of diagnostic processes and medical knowledge, it is rather a re-enactment of the method of deduction that the doctor should follow in the process of diagnosis when the relevant imputes have already been decided. The cyber-diagnostician could be eventually in-corporate within bodies so that continual checks can be made especially of immunity levels that can allow for prompt action to deal with infection, malfunction, as well as overall diet/ nutrient requirements: a sort of over all vitality-check. Health regimen would, thus, acquire a more concrete form, and the term preventive medicine would actually have some material basis.

I suppose it is important to understand the distinction between synthesis and simulation. "By synthesis of an artificially intelligent system is meant the development of a system capable of producing intelligent results or exhibiting intelligent behavior of one kind or another, without any pretense that the methods used bear any resemblance to those used by human beings." (George, 1969: 74) For example, if a computer is programmed to integrate a mathematical function, it will do iterations adding bits of area to approximate the result, instead of the human method of solving it through pre-developed technics and formulas. No one argues that simulation is better than synthesis. In the previous example, they arrive at approximately similar results. Rather, simulations set higher goals then achieving the same result: "Simulations, on the other hand, which is a particular case of synthesis, not only attempts to achieve the same ends, but also claims to produce it them in a way similar to the way in which they are produced by human beings." (George, 1969: 74)

In this regard, simulated systems are closer to replacing the human factor than simply synthetic ones since they also bear a close resemblance to human decision making patterns: logic and reason. The use of simulation, then, is not only to solve problems by technical means, but to

---

9 AEGIS home page is located at: http://www.aegis.com/
[10]Cine Med home page at: http://www.cine-med.com/cinemed/vrweb.html general virtual reality.

mirror the process of human cognition, thinking, learning to become: a kind of logic cyber-preceptor device, that can eventually be in synapse with brains: as through the development of wetware. So technological advances can be seen to have a three-fold basis: the development of software, being the programming of code that establishes the operations of machines and their interfaces with humans; hardware, the very material construction of the machine; and now wetware, direct links of human/machine. Expert systems as used today tend to have more of a synthetic or supplemental character since for the most part they do not always mirror the diagnostic methods of physicians, and are statistically determined.

The diagnostic procedure through a computerized expert system requires that the doctor will enter the appropriate data, and that it does not read its own data or inputs from the body of the patient. Nevertheless, they still require the presence of the physician. However with the advent of preceptor devices that can read instantaneously measurements from the body, the medical practice could be limited to research that would continually establish new techniques, methods, and devices that would be miniaturized and eventually incorporated in medical practice or directly linked to cybernetic bodies. I will demonstrate how medicine can operate without doctors, how indeed medical practice will necessarily be refigured by current technological advances especially through the advent of preceptor devices. It is necessary to determine whether our infatuation with technical solutions do indeed offer better medical practice for post-humans, whether indeed the cyborgian transmutation, the adding of technical devices to monitor and regulate human function, offers increased levels of livability even in the face of the degeneration of familiar environments, and the depletion of traditional resources (by familiar I mean environments that we have already adapted to, and by traditional energy recourses I refer to those that are conventionally used, i.e., oil, gas). Even if we are confronted with such transformations, will it be possible to conceive of a medicine without doctors? What kinds of conceptual problems do arise, and how can solutions be found?

2. On A Medicine Without Doctors: Research On The Limits Of The Visible.

> In order to counter this vision one must actively and strategically seek alternative spatial and creative logistics, social and cultural configurations. If such creative flexibility is critically foregrounded in current research agendas, cyberspace will indeed become a site of considerable cultural promise, and a locale for a new post-organic anthropology. (Tomas, 1994: 46)

The question I pose initially is how can medicine be transformed to be flexible in the advent of new structures of expertise, of more equalized information flows (the possibility of informed and resistant patients), and of an altered basis for authority as accreditation, especially with the re-thinking of the university that is no longer an enclosure of knowledge but a medium of information generation and verification. These changes, which effect all social institutions, become more visible and clear through the medical example. However, I would anticipate similar kinds of issues to develop for other institutions: legal and governmental. I primarily focus on the medical example and note what changes I see in the info-structure. Thus, I begin my analysis with the possibility of a medicine without doctors in the conventional sense since they can be substituted by computer DB. Then, only researchers would be needed to expand the current knowledge base. So, would the doctor as practitioner be displaced by the expert computer system that is more reliable, cheaper, and easier to distribute? that potentially can be integrated with the organic body?

To really comprehend the argument, one needs to understand not just the economic forces operating, but also the ways in which information flows have been (re)established, so that previous power dipoles can no longer be supported. In other words, no "true" masters of knowledge can ever exist in telematic societies since there is too much information to master anyhow and no real point in mastering it all. One can conceive as future experts the computer-human inter-links that have enhanced memory and processing capacities. However, they could become exclusive to the privileged technocrats if provisions are not made so that the technologies used will not remain in their total grasp. This interfacing of human and artifact, including the advent of wetware, is a product of cybernetics. Cybernetics, in terms of information, is "the science of control and communication in the animal and the machine" (Rosie, 1969: 145), a way of mastering the code that governs them. Information theory (which structures the link between human and machine codes) has become the basis of understanding and communication, of determining what the signal is and what is mere noise. (Rosie, 1969) Consequently, information has been isolated from the semantics of sender/ receiver because it has been structured to render meaning via the form of the signal that needs to be decoded by the proper decoder. (Woolley, 1994) Information theory appears to have simplified the complexities of interpretation through the process of digitalization (a series of on/ off, in binary). The distinctive feature of the signal is the pattern of wave that is transmitted, and the medium through which it is distributed and received.

Information as signaled is simply the reception of on/ off, and ignores the context of the message for its encoded form. The on/ off signal of information theory is simplistic, but pertains to the fact that the content of information can only be established in context of many bits of information woven together to form a portrayal, picture, form, syntax, language, spoken word, depending of the type of the signal. The content of information always needs to be encoded and decoded in contrast to the form, which is structured as a series of on/off. The on/off, in signaling information through any medium such as light, radio waves, electrical pulses, bio-electricity, is different from the content of the message itself, which can never be reduced to such simplistic default encodings. The relation, I have established, between form and content in information theory, resembles the connection of structuralism to deconstruction. This opposition of form to content is problematic in either the setting of information or literary theory since they tend to ignore the context in which the message appears, who its intended reader/ decoder is, and how it can be misconstrued. Information is powerful only when it is discoursified in such a fashion as to grant the (intended or unintended) receiver of the message the surplus of insight and knowledge into his/ her own situation. So information must always be situated to avoid the oversimplified argument of what is more important form or content.

It is significant to situate medical information and knowledge, and to understand how the two relate. Knowledge is intricately ordered information, and therefore cannot be interpreted in many fashions. The distinctions between knowledge, information, data, then, are the degrees of freedom to be mediated and inter-fused with other bits of data, information, knowledge. In general, medical information and data can largely be distributed by policy makers in the floor of congress, by various activist organizations, by the media, by specialist journals, by universities, and all can propose various strategies for interpreting it. For example, what do low HIV infection rates among heterosexuals vs. homosexuals mean in Britain in view of the fact that globally 70% of HIV infection is by heterosexual means. Knowledge on the other hand is mediated primarily by university structures that are granted the authority to surveil it, and guarantee its proper social reproduction. Knowledge, thus, situates information in context and tests the validity of various interpretations, to establish and verify it with regard to all data or inputs.

Thus, the cybernetic form of medicine will depend on the future of the university (if it is private or public, if it funded by corporations, if it is regulated by a governmental body, etc.). The future of medical practice will thus change if the status of expertise changes and how it is acquired. The structure of the doctor/ patient dyad will have to change along with the birth of expert systems and other such structures (virtual reality, net-pages, user-groups, to name a few) and with the increased availability of medical information and. knowledge, i.e., the potential of a cyber-university. It would then be a matter of policy whether doctors are required and necessary to prescribe standard treatments or if an expert system diagnosis would suffice. Taking it a step further: the potential incorporation of health monitoring technologies within our bodies would make going to the doctor for a checkup sound archaic, making all of us into cyborgs as mandatory vaccination dealt with certain forms of disease in the turn of the century.

Some questions remain: will the increase in information also provide us with the skill to determine what information is valid and the ability to determine which treatments or device implants are best and why? will that require experts or other expert systems or simply higher education standards or bio-consumer watchdogs? will everyone have access to the same databases? will they be free or charged? When all issues are raised, it becomes clear that the future will be in some ways as class determined as the present if not more since a lot is at stake. For example, medical decisions on treatment could be easily determined by the level of information and technology purchased by the level of medical technologies that one can afford by the longevity of one's life and working capacity and so....

If information is redistributed and if institutions cannot (as they cannot to date) maintain clear and regulatable borders in cyberspace (other than parental filters, screening the net of unsuitable information), and if technologically determined borders are not completely fixed but permeable, then it would be possible to have a system that would become less class determined, that would be able to overcome unequal holds on information and knowledge. Bureaucracies have maintained a hold on powerful information (for example the culture of secrecy surrounding classified US documents), and the technologies necessary to process it into meaningful knowledge. Such hold is questioned today, arriving at the fact that a lot of US classified documents that are over 10 years old would be declassified, making this very culture of secrecy seem absurd.[11] It is possible to conceive how cyberspace can facilitate the breaking down of traditional barriers of time/space, nation, race, gender ... but not class at least without an externally mediated network of free and informed sources that may be governmental or subsidized? Maybe the reason for the existence of a participatory governmentality would be to guarantee and check information flows that are provided by technological innovations, medicine, media, universities, as a means through which an openness and transparency can be safeguarded in the interest of all....

The fundamental requirement for cybernetic devices to displace their human counterparts in such positions as the doctor-practitioner is to have the ability to perceive and learn without direct human involvement. They would have to develop strategies of independence that are not limited by human intelligence in order to surpass it and its blind spots. At this point, machine code/ language could be truly self generative and reproducing (as the elementary forms of computer viruses and their transmutations suggest). One can understand the real anxiety behind sci-fi humor: *infected with a computer virus*. The question is what if, especially when wetware is developing? We have started interrogating our privilege as the only planet with life in the universe, along with our the position on the top of the chain of life, maybe now is also the time to realize that the conceptual defaults that produced such assertions and distinctions (Aliens/ Human/ Animal) are problematic that the fundamental separation of life and artifact is not self evident as well as other such bipolar conceptions, that organic and inorganic are not *essentially* opposed. As such a fuzzy undertaking (which results from an application of *fuzzy logic*), one can imagine the evolution (!?) of new line of preceptor/ learner devices that can communicate in both human and digital code. A delusive dream or nightmare?

---

[11] From *Independent* newspaper article on April 3, 1997, page 21. "US report reveals: secrets need a short life cycle."

Before I begin describing how cyber-preceptors are established as the new or final (?) frontier, it would aid my argument to clearly delimit what is meant by perception and how it ties to information or data gathered through senses or inputs that are integrated into clear pictures and representations of 'things'; how, indeed, stimuli are always linked to their interpretations. Perception is roughly the process that classifies the new and recognizes familiar stimuli. (George, 1969) The process is determined by a pattern recognition that dissembles the whole into parts and establishes key features that serve as identifiers or gestalts. Identifiers help in the establishment of conceptual categories that are given names (addresses) to aid the process of recollection and communication. Language is already a simulator of concepts that humans use in classifying and recalling stimuli. (George, 1969) The opposition of simulation and surveillance seems problematic, since surveillance/ discipline/ observation is required for discoursification and discourse is always already an elementary form of simulation. In this specific context, linguistic nuances mirror the degrees of understanding and complexity that a particular culture has, whether the language or code take the form of oral-written accounts, digital signaling, Morse signs, Pascal, C++, assembly, or even gestures.

Language as a medium of interconnection and circulation of information is essential to learning whether it takes the form of verbal, written, chemical, technological codes. Learning is the process of adapting to new perceptual and conceptual givens as they become formed by further signals or stimuli, so that novel information is derived from the data as reflecting the signals or stimuli. This information can then be systematized into knowledges or more generally conceptual theories, paradigms, epistemes, world-views. Higher levels of integration have been established upon a greater separation from data and may be illusive the more they become remote. Maybe such levels of integration would become irrelevant. I suppose that the connection between stimuli for humans and data/ signals for devices is clear, and that they are already structured in parallel to facilitate their interface. The construction of thinking, imagining, perceiving cybernetic systems capable of developing their own code, that hopefully will be close to a cognizant human language, is feasible. In fact high-level programming languages (Pascal, C++) have already attempted to reflect human syntax in order to facilitate their learning. From a hardware point of view, both human and computers operate on forms of electric current that can make their direct inter-linking possible.

Another coding system that I have largely ignored although it is relevant to cyborgs is the genetic one. The prospect of using the DNA as building blocks for micro-computers is a reality since genes are in their basic formulation information storers. Genetic processors can make current hi-tech computers even laptops appear large. These genetic processors would be extremely small in scale which enhances the possibility of their incorporation (as memory implants or data storers) within cyborgs. The mapping out the human genome is real, and the potential applications of genetic technologies can range from genetic enhancement (gene therapy) to engineering generations of cyborgs. The possibility (whether ethical or not) is intriguing, and does point to the need of public decision making on such issues. Genetics is a field that is riddled with ethical dilemmas. However it is capable of concretizing our grasp of organic forms and their manufacture. I doubt that genetic control = total control since we are shaped by more than our genes. However, the desire to fix behavioral patterns to genetic causes is problematic and reflects the desire to unconditionally contain, monitor, define the Other/ enemy whatever shape it may take. I will consider the implications of technological innovation to our already cybernetic societies to indulge in a futurology that may reflect a time not as distant as it now may appear by working on the

advent of the cyber-preceptor and how it would impact the structure of medicine.

> Now they are preparing the way for the *automatons of perception*, for the innovation of artificial vision, delegating the analysis of objective reality to a machine...(Virilo, 1994:59)

3. The Cyber-Preceptor: The New or Final Frontier?

One may wonder what is next: medicine without doctors; devices that can perceive, think, learn, and communicate with humans; posthumans that are not distinct from machines; the birth of cyborgs? Well, these are not new objectives and their implications would be wide. I will not argue about the human ability to produce or not such devices that only history will determine. It would, however, be interesting to see the ramifications of such technologies upon human structures, focusing of course primarily on medicine. The vision to create a preceptor/learner machine is not new. It emanates from our understanding of biological and behavioral systems. Clearly developments in information and signal processing for computers have helped neurologists understand and even model the behaviors of neurons and the brain. The challenge, thus, has been twofold to determine how to design technologies that "employ processes and techniques and accomplish functions which hitherto have existed only in living systems" (Steele, 1995: 55) to establish the field of bionics, and to further integrate biological matter with technology as in the field of neuro-cybernetics.

The revolution in human models of perception has occurred when research on brains and computers converged, the point being: the way research problems have been defined. (Walter, 1969) In constructing learner machines, one would be able to delineate how systems of feedback work in human brains. The 'reflex learner' for example is "sensitive to rewarded relations between stimuli it receives and the responses it produces." (Pask, 1969) Further, it is able to evaluate and solve situations in which it finds itself. The preceptor/learner device produces a technical simulation of the world, a perceptive field that we have to enter as foreigners. Even if machines are mirrored upon the human, they always remain radically other and require one to adapt to them. The distinction between cyber-preceptors and regular processors is that the latter ones require inputs in order to process the data being fed by human operators, whereas the former have their own sensory stimuli that they can directly discern and interpret.

Cyber- preceptors, for example, would be capable of adapting to continuous stimulus (habituation), tuning out what is irrelevant or unimportant, processing information tirelessly at incredible speeds, adapting to new situations, and inventing strategies to problem-solve. They would be capable of unbelievable mental and physical feats, all in all, the super or extra human-computer at our service or our absolute master? The fear that we would be dominated by our own constructions is not new, and some would interpret any related problems that arise as "god's" retribution for our arrogance. Again maybe cyber-preceptors will not be that simple to invent and would always be delimited by our intelligence as creators. Or maybe indeed technology and humans will be co-evolving and fusing in a symbiotic system and the question is not really about domination but of facilitation. It is up to us to figure which story line we would like to produce as our futures.

It is important to understand that a preceptor devise whether attached to a mega processor or not can augment our realities, and are not just simulations of our reality. "Augmented and simulated realities represent different approaches to interacting with virtual worlds. Rather than a virtual world created out of virtual illusion, augmented realities are created out of the stuff of the real world." (Kellogg, 1994:421) Augmented preceptor devices already exist such as those that provide pilots/ and other soldiers the ability to see at night. Also different organisms have different perceptual fields, and use different ranges then us, who are extremely visually centered, and perceive only a fraction of the electromagnetic spectrum (the visual spectrum). Perceiving color is an illusion. So instrumentation has become indispensable to all human endeavors not only medicine. With the intrusion of technologies into our perceptual field, it has become increasingly difficult to distinguish a simulation from the real. An example would be particle physics when one is observing and studying things that cannot be readily visible by humans even with their perceptual prosthetics.

Consequently, the margin of error in determining what is facilitated reality verses a virtual representation or simulation is wide, and hard to determine or impossible to always determine. Thus, technological simulation or augmented realities come at a cost of the real and establish an irreducible distance between simulation/representation and substance (such distance has always existed: now it is difficult to ignore). When cyber-preceptor and cyber-learner devices are attached to expert systems, the process of knowing would clearly be transformed. It could be that our enhanced consciousness are read directly into computers that may then be verified and/ or upgraded against their perhaps augmented perceptual fields that would be more valid or more enhanced than the (post)human-real. We would be called to adapt beyond the grasp of our human understanding. Maybe these cyber-preceptors/ learners could be an extrasensory feature added to us as prosthetic, so that we move to the next level of perceptive integration, the next stage in the game of knowing, perceiving, communicating.

Enhanced cyborgic perception would mark the end to subjective/ objective claims of completely distinct knowledges. In fact, this opposition is clearly constructed upon the necessity of a human observer/ actor. When a human observes, the findings can be granted the status of objectivity if they are presented in a characteristic form (presently the scientific), and if they can be verified by other mostly human observers. Then, they are accepted as valid until otherwise determined. When a human acts or interferes, then his/her justifications of his/her actions are termed subjective, and are put under the lens of observation as such a subject is always subjected to a "sovereign" gaze (even if such gaze is internal as the superego) that always asks for an apologia. Observation and objectification have become the predominate mode of knowledge generation under the guise of science. For each knowledge system, standards have been determined through time, further observation, and general consensus or enforcement that one has to measure up against: in the first case methods, in the second ethics and both are constantly contested. This objective/ subjective split is determined primarily by our limits of perception, and thus when enhanced, it would be undermined. In a hyper-stimulated world, where no perceptual filters (biologically determined or not) are worn, the contrasts that we see as constitutive of concrete objects, as distinct and separable from the rest soup of info (background), would be indiscernible. Perceptual contrast (as binary opposition) is a visual illusion that has dominated western thought since it is dependent upon the structure of our eyes that perceive only visual spectrum, and upon the wiring of our brains.

Enhanced perception is already present in our societies. When these preceptor devices are linked with processors and/or humans, a revolution of the knowledge field is inevitable (for example, revolutions or reform of medicine in recent time has been dependent upon the invention of perceptual technologies: the microscope, that was key in the development of germ theory). Maybe then it would be no longer a question of human or machine. Maybe cyborgs mark the point where the question of domination and mastery of information, knowledge, technology would be irrelevant if not class bound. We are called to evolve at our own choice and with our own prosthetics that can be tailor-made. Consequently, "evolution is more than the survival of the fittest. And participant evolution can make fit the adventurous, the self-chosen unfit and probably improve the qualities of life more effectively, even in the long run, than just waiting for the less fit to become extinct. Let us pay homage to those adventurous fish who ventured unto the land. Without them we would not be here. Their less adventurous cousins are fit and still survive today, in water." (Clynes, 1995) This vision of evolution, as not just the survival of the fittest but as self-chosen destiny, is problematic since it is difficult to choose when one does not know and not everyone is offered the choice. Cyborgs are supposedly the adventurous and poly-morphous fish of the future that can choose their tailor-made prosthetics, so that they can enhance their survival on earth, in space, under water.... Many questions remain unanswered and even un-formulated about what kind of future it might be, for whom, in whose interest, and how it can be best shaped today.

I expect it has become more clear who would be the main benefactor of cyborgian transmutations. It is certain it will not just be the adventurous cyborgs, transgressing new terrains at their will or not: the most benefits will go to the technocrats that will pile their money/ blips and continue to design new technologies for the naive, adventurous, sick, or optimistic. To maintain a lead in the cyborg-market, it would of course be necessary to acquire, hold, and process the most relevant information in order to be able to design future prosthetics for demanding cyborg-consumers who need to survive in an increasingly corrupted, unwelcoming ecology. Their knowledge base has been a simple fusion of medicine and cybernetics. It would be of paramount interest to cyborg-consumers to determine "the differences between restorative, normalizing, reconfiguring, enhancing, and degrading cyborg technologies [which] seem particularly important in ethical terms." (Gray, 1995a: 3) The political irony is that differences between types of cyborgic applications apart from being of ethical interest, would be class bound, and the site of resistant cyborgic manifestos. In cyber-worlds, human life may lose its value on the market since economies will not be human-driven, especially when cybernetic systems become capable of designing and producing their own future generations without the supervision of humans, using outdated cyborg-versions for their trial runs to acquire precious data from an ever more un-welcoming real world.

IV. Political Ironies: An Afterthought

> Liberation rests on the construction of the consciousness, the imaginative apprehension, of oppression, and so of possibility. The cyborg is a matter of fiction and lived experience that changes what counts as woman's experience in the late twentieth century. This is a struggle over life and death, but the boundary between science fiction and social reality is an optical illusion. (Haraway, 1991: 149)

Where else should I begin then the trap of futurism, especially when the picture is always presented at its best. To be iconoclastic is not original and does not contribute to the shaping of that very future-present as their separation keeps diminishing. The collapse between simulation and reality are central to the cyborgic transition: a kind of necessary psychosis or delusion, so that we can speed up to tomorrow and ignore the process of getting there. Our situation resembles that of the driver fixating on the fact that the vehicle is accelerating, and forgetting to scrutinize the change in the scenery, forgetting even what remains the same. Politics is really the art of representing the future, of painting pictures that can be communicated, of performing gestures that may or may not signify what they intend. The advent of simulation marks an end to ideologies that have been supported by representational structures; thus, the political game of interaction is altered alongside the case of medicine.

Without the doctor, the political representative, the university instructor, social interaction does lose at least some of its theatrical character. Nietzsche has first marked the loss of theatricality in modern societies, and the prevalence of a Socratic mode of intercommunication: didactic, dialectic, and critical. (Nietzsche, 1956) Theatrics have made modern stories interesting for at least their entertainment value: the lecture theater, the media scene, the spectacle of science. The effect of animation has taken over, i.e., the making of the impossible/ possible through simulation. Societies, thus, become their self-generating codes since identity has been determined through the language that is presently destabilized so that we will act out the plot to its very failure. Am I just being pessimistic? Not if we measure the possible against the expectations building up for the future, the advertisement that goes with the promise of change, and the underling motivators for change.

What results from this failure to apprehend, from the lack of opportunity to reflect since that is considered passé (one rather projects and gambles) is the enjoyment of the present impossible ideological moves. Corporations, which are indisputably the economic motivators of change, promise to operate with respect for social interests as if they have realized that social interests are identical with their own (or the term social has lost its distance from individual) and thus will work for the long run by putting aside short term profit. Or that workers' unions are no longer necessary because of "enlightened" management. These claims do appear dubious to say the least. But let me examine how we enjoy our ideological innocence (which is not always equivalent to false consciousness) that tends to prevail in the present political scene. Enjoyment has always been of paramount political significance since the stakes of politics are not in the today but in the tomorrow, and to convince us that through their planning tomorrow will fix yesterday or the reverse that today is not as good as yesterday so tomorrow needs to be rescued from the present.

In each case scenario the left and right determine their positions according to their ideological investments. Therefore, the "fall" of communism, could be interpreted in two fashions: a. there was no longer a need for Communist states to exist as separate from socially enlightened European ones; b. communism failed because it does not work and never will, because it does not take into account individual incentive. Whatever view one adopts it is clearly shaped by ideology. So, "today more than ever, in the midst of the scoundrel time we live in, the duty of the Left [and Right] is to keep alive the memory of all the lost causes, of all the shattered dreams and hopes attached to leftist [and rightist] projects [such as the war on drugs, poverty...]." (Zizek, 1991: 271) And clearly, we would most be remembered by these failures that are the symptoms/ sources of our fantasies, and the surplus of our enjoyments. (Zizek, 1989) Forgetting our failures can be tragic especially if we are not willing to challenge our position, and it is certain that political gains are always the product of resistance and activism; even if those concepts need to be re-invented to suit our contexts and to develop our concepts of sociality. No one ever hands down rights and rarely acts in socially "enlightened" ways.

Consequently, technology and science need to be continually contested to expose them as political/ ideological forms "of knowledge reflective of power." (Stepan, 1993: 187) "The romantic notions of science as a pursuit of pure, unadulterated 'objective' truth, with the scientist working in isolation from mundane reality -- like a hermit, trying against impossible odds to understand some objective reality -- has become dangerously untenable." (Third World Network, 1993: 485) In our heightened interconnected world, higher costs are attached to the maintenance of expertise and power, raising the stakes in the shaping of knowledge. Put in plain: corporations are interested to invest and improve technologies and knowledges that can help them profit and predict future trends, so that they can have a stronger-hold on the market (resulting in larger revenues and capital), and as a consequence to have a greater influence upon government. An escape from the political game, as embedded in the pursuit of knowledge, is impossible even when such gestures are made in the "interest" of objective knowledge. These gestures are feeble attempts to hide the will to power. It is important to determine how to structure the interconnections between institutions of surveillance, expertise, entertainment, information with sociality as a model for the foundation of an ethical/ activist type of politics, based on direct participation and transparency.

The irony is placed in the fact that participation can become another theatrical display, that appeases the public because of its entertainment value, as with present governmental elections, while allowing the power-holders to continue their work uninterrupted in the meantime. The classic US example: how has the tobacco industry managed to retain itself as legitimate business for so long in its blatant soliciting of youth by presenting smoking as an independent person's activity? how could the tobacco industry provide campaign contributions to congressional candidates legitimately? could anyone rule out that action against them has been delayed so long after the addictiveness of nicotine is established because of their congressional endorsements? Even if the market of cigarettes is declining in the US, it is rising in other countries that do not have as strict medical policies. Thus, international action is probably the only effective means of addressing nicotine addiction on a global scale.

It would be the over-indulgent ideological failure of the present optimism and trust in technologies and technocrats not to empower people with information, with the ability to critique, and with the faculty to directly participate in the political game. The age of revolution is succeeded by the age of simulation. The revolutionary age has been interested in absolutes, and has presented revolution as the only means of "ridding itself from the muck of ages and become fitted to found society anew." (Marx, 1991: 95) These ideologies of revolution still reside among us (versions of state nationalism, socialism...) along with ideologies of older times that have returned with a vengeance (religious fundamentalism): all asking for more blood shed. The question is how can simulation be mapped so that it leads to a dynamic symbiosis, beyond the dualisms of individual-collective not to an organic whole, but rather to a cybernetic coalition of differences?

1. On Collaboration And Diversity: A Critique of Fixed Grounds.

> And if governmentalization is really this movement concerned with subjugating individuals in this very reality of social practice by mechanisms of power that appeal to a truth, I will say that critique is the movement through which the subject gives itself the right to question truth concerning its power effects and to question power about its discourse of truth. Critique will be the art of voluntary inservitude, of reflective indocility. This essential function of critique would be that of desubjectification in the game of what one could call, in a word, the politics of truth.(Foucault, 1996: 386)

The status of ideology needs to be examined with its relation to governmentality and critique before more symbiotic and resistant forms of collaboration and diversity can be established to facilitate change. Ideologies (revolutionary or otherwise) are the employment and development of strategies/ maneuvers that allow the gain or retainment of a strong hold upon the shaping of governmentality. A good example in terms of medicine would be the construction of a medico-scientific triumph over tuberculosis that cannot be said to truly have happened since TB at present does not have a cure, but rather rates of infection and susceptibility have declined in "advanced" societies. The medico-scientific narrative of triumph over TB has resulted in the situating of science and medicine as central to policy making (for example the hygiene party as a response to TB in France). Ideological claims should always be put under great scrutiny to determine the circuit of power-knowledge relations, which can be promoted either as an all cure or as a means of preserving the status quo. Grand revolutionary visions (for example the scientific reform of medicine with its calumniation in the TB triumph) along with prolific nationalisms (did the French, German, English, or Americans solved the TB crisis best?) are coming to an end because it is no longer in the interest of a more global market (of knowledge and expertise as well as commodities) to have conflicts and borders (increased taxation of information or products, and obstructions of circulation from one region to the other) that impede the distribution of commerce and profiting.

As such, conflict (whose ultimate manifestation is war) has been deemed necessary if it is in the interest of business, of course in the name of democracy (gulf war) and domestic peace (war on drugs, poverty, AIDS). The answer to whose business would be profiting most is obvious here: the strongest military and ally-wise, or who has the ability to have a greater impact on mainstream ideology. However, with nationalism's necessary end arises a refusal to end by the ones who have benefited or felt secured by the nation's existence (as an instance: the latest upsurges of nationally/ racially motivated violence in Germany or Holland).[12] The motivator of such spurs of nationalism and religious fundamentalism is the perception of a definite lack within the symbolic. (Zizek, 1994b) The nation-state is going, yet what will take it's place does not appear to be self-evident or clear. The nation-state's birth has been mirrored in pictorial representations of sociological coherence as an organic whole in a body whose divisions have been always functionally integrated, explicit, and scientific. (Hobbes, 1965)

With the realization that the body may no longer be a functional, but a fictional totality, i.e., it has never been such, state romances that have assumed unity through bodily ideality are also coming to an end. Their ideological investments are no longer prevalent not because "the postmodern nation state is certainly more of a cyborg, than it is a machine with a soul" (Gray & Mentor, 1996), but because decisive coherence and singularity are exposed as always been coercive and ideologically invested in their representations (since they have been racially, sexually... mediated). The organic model of the state is formed as a coherent entity only in exclusion of certain non-functional members: the Mad, the Criminal, the Hysteric, the Leper, the TB or AIDS infected, the Immigrant, the Black, the Indian, the Woman, the Other.... An attempt to arrive at a pluralistic, but not indifferent solution that is primarily iconoclastic, and has an ultra-skeptical attitude towards any ideological claims is central. Consensus "is not a criterion of truth, is not a standard value, is not am index of moral or ethical appropriateness, is not a requisite for co-operation, is not

---

[12] *Independent* newspaper article, April 3, 1997 page 17, "Turks fear anti-Islamic hate behind murders."

a communal imperative for a just social order, is not, in and of itself, an appropriate ideal." (Rescher, 199) A discourse that establishes notions of validity upon a consensus is problematic. Consensus can never grant veracity. Along with the model of the state as organic, the discourses that supplied such model of coherence are also under scrutiny.

The nation state's legitimating expert base, science, is presently becoming more questioned and contested. The rise of science studies as well as the need for a more "public understanding" of science mirror such pressure. With the term science in this context, I mean the establishment of a certain set of natural laws that govern phenomena through a singular/ universal method of observation and codification of data and information, through standardized modes of inference. The privileged position of science in the nation state can be determined by the fact that every other discourse has desired to attain scientific status. The status of science came to be equivalent with a legitimate form of knowledge that produced/ demonstrated truth, that could then have a say in the dealings of power. I have already talked about the making of a scientific medicine at the tern of the century with the development of more reliable diagnostics, a standardization of practice and method as to resemble science. However, the motivating force for change in medicine and elsewhere is not a more diligent application of scientific observation per se, but rather major innovations in technology. Maybe what has been termed as modern scientific advances are just the product of the development in instrumentation, which always has been of key importance, but whose contribution has been underrated.

The privileged position of science as a form of knowledge is established by its baptizing of engineering (as the umbrella term for the development and invention of technologies) as an application of scientific principles and laws. In the example of medicine, the increasing dependence of medical advances upon technological ones is an emergent reality, when most claims to the establishment of universal and coherent scientific laws that govern the body appear romantic if not impossible. The importance of technology has risen because medical advancements have become dependent upon innovation as it can be illustrated by the birth of cyborgs and their adaptation as the third millennium medical products. The key question to ask is how are these changes promoted/ commercialized by impossible (when they are measured against the real) ideologies (for example the idea of a global village), and how can the game of governmentality be played in such a way as to safeguard openness against absolutism, to establish collaboration as the basis for knowledge-production along with a respect for diversity. How could these concepts (collaboration and diversity) be incorporated to mean not in an ideological sense, but rather to help us move out of the imperative rhetoric of ideology?

An ideological structure is perpetuated by certain claims to power as established upon the spectacle of truth or demonstration, and the establishment of their inherent presuppositions as fixed, axiomatic, and universal grounds. These demonstrations are acceptable in so far as they appease the public's curiosity, and when the claims made can be supportable or replicable. So a key to a post-ideological frame of mind is to have a critical attitude towards any knowledges that claim to be truth or to be demonstrably the only truth, and to always destabilize the connection of power with fixed knowledge or expertise as an anchor. It is important to understand how are the establishment of knowledge- grounds is always ideological.

A fixed ground or anchor is established as such because it is perceived to be true and in fact it is (re)produced through discursive practices that will it to be true, because it is suitable to a ruling class of individuals. Knowledges are not ideologically fixed if they do not claim to have a complete grasp of truth. Truth in the absolute does not exist. Rather one can perceive the real only in situational contexts, and in a perspective that establishes degrees of veracity combined with uncertainties about method, instrumentation, approach. The appearance of a singular incontestable truth is always ideologically constructed to appear as secure knowledge. It is because the persons whose interests it serves are in such a position as to perform the demonstration of truth in a ritual fashion and to convince whoever wishes to be totally convinced. Such demonstrations only materialize though the veil of truth the will to power. Knowledge should never lose its provisional status, and should not be the only basis for decision making. Decisions must be informed by knowledge and guided by ethics.

Policy making needs to be freed from the total grasp and claims of experts. This would allow people to share power and have a larger stake in society, with of course increased responsibility in the shaping of the world. Then, gross inequalities can have the prospect of being diminished, and the overall global standard of life raised. The key is to abolish all types of discrimination in terms of race, gender, class, nationality, sexuality, and so forth, and to acknowledge as a vibrant part of the economy, work that has been previously underpaid or not acknowledged such as housework (Davis, 1983). An example, as it relates to gender, is that the value of work done by conventionally female professionals, for example, speech therapists who have been underpaid in Britain as compared to other professionals (just because they tend to be females? and their clients cannot speak?).[13] When these jobs are acknowledged as a growing part of the economy, then investments in technologies that can assist will be made so that work is less dependent upon human factors. In the inability to recognize (through salary) such occupations as legitimate forms of employment, one runs the risk of creating an enslaved/ dependent class of individuals including the young. I am not certain if the development of private property is the key source of inequality. I think discrimination, as the establishment of a secure difference between powerful, legitimate, *Universal* in contrast to non exceptional *Particular*, is the shortcoming of all

---

[13] *Independent* newspaper article April 4, 1997 page 7. "Victory in historic fight to show equal worth for women"

ideologies. Any pretense to arrive at a certain, incontestable a priori standard of truth that is self-evident or common sensical can only be such through undetected ideological investments.

Discrimination does not always take the form of coercion and overt oppression, but can be veiled through the lack of opportunity to transcend one's given social situation; as a result, social mobility would be the most important factor in the making of a less class bound world. Discrimination (i.e., the establishment of an a priori difference) is not only a direct but also an indirect means of asserting mainstream ideological investments. Medical practice and policy during the early AIDS epidemic as well as during the TB crisis have been tainted by discriminatory practices against immigrants, the poor, or isolated individuals whose families did not have the means or who were simply uninterested in taking care of them. When no *a priori* differences are established, then we can move to a collaborative frame of mind that respects the differences between groups and individuals among themselves, that is willing to negotiate ways of interaction and inter-permeation in order to figure out a more symbiotic movement.

Marx's assertion that the community is the only place where an individual can be free is extremely problematic (Marx & Engels, 1991) if that is taken to mean a complete abolition of the self as separable entity in favor of communal ideologies. I suppose his assertion has arisen from the determination of property as the sole cause of social inequality, and individuality is thus determined by property as separable from community. The mediation and acquisition of property are what establishes the distinction of private/ public through law. Although I do agree with the overall analysis, I do not think that privileging the community over the individual is the answer or the opposite privileging the individual over the community. I think it is essential to move out of this false dilemma and to realize the importance for the existence of individuals and communities without setting one as more important than the other, as the exemplary, universal standard. It is historically establishable that communities have also been capable of atrocities not just separable individuals. To blame individualist thinking for all social ills is as problematic as saying that a communal logic can solve them (examples: US McCarthyism, Former Soviet Stalinism).

The key is to move beyond default thinking and to constantly problematize theoretical defaults since they are the result of privileging the *Universal* over particulars, and since they are always ideologically motivated. To construct a governmentality that always acknowledges the limitations of any adapted line of inquiry or policy, but that strives to find a best fit, by taking into account all available information, and by being certain that all such information is heard. The only way to become sure that all points of view are considered is to have an inclusive structure that permeates fixed borders, that allows for what may have been previously unthought or silenced to become heard and accommodated. This inclusive structure should have as main directives: the rising the global standard of living, the respect for life and ecology, the formation of symbiotic structures of governing.

Ideologies are produced in narrative fashion and stabilize themselves through a historical mode that becomes foundational, regarded as valid, and central to the claims to truth and power. Thus, it is important to destabilize this historical mode of operation, to allow for the unmasking of claims to power and their totalizing prevalence, to construct genealogical and archeological modes of analysis that provide a critical re-evaluation of these historical claims. In the example of the medical triumph over TB, can such event be verified through the treatments that have been prescribed? their effectiveness? what did the rhetoric of a medico-scientific triumph veil? what other possible answers can be given to the historical record? do they appear to have more validity and be supportable by this record? and so on.... The construction of an ideological singularity is determined by the unidirectional relation between cause and effect that becomes indisputable, that tends to ignore other situational factors, which also shape the event.

To move beyond ideological games, one has to always retain a critical attitude, to always search for alternate answers, and to not stabilize upon only one determinate source of change or course of action: rather to adapt flexible movements. A historicophilosophical frame of mind is indispensable in the unmasking of ideological claims. Thus, the construction of history should be denuded from the requirements of a narrative as a progression from past, present, to future, which can be easily manipulated to fit present interests and should always be in dialogue. We need to move away from emancipatory rhetoric such as: "We should be content with providence and with the course of human affairs as a whole, which does not begin with good and end with evil, but develops gradually from the worse to the better, and each individual is for his part called upon by nature itself to contribute towards this progress to the best of his abilities." (Kant, 1970a: 234) We need to construct a history that is freed from ideological directives, that can be re-conceived as dromological, i.e., in a continual movement, and that refuses to be fixed in any one ideological position.

2. On Movement: What If Historical Time Is Not Unidirectional.

> The cutting loose of time from sequence, and consequently from human identity, constitutes the third wave of postmodernism. Time still exists in a cultural postmodernism, but it no longer functions as a continuum along which human action can meaningfully be plotted. (Hayles, 1990: 279)

Linear progression or succession is linked to our conception of time. Time in this context is simply a narrative device that has been manipulated by novelists such as James Joyce, who in the making of a modern *Ulysses* imploded the connection of real and novel time. *Ulysses*, which is a fairly long novel that has a modernist theme, mirrors the events of an ordinary day, less than 24 hours. So the time it takes to read the novel is more than the time it took to perform it, and in certain sections it is measured to read exactly as long as it takes to perform. With this implosion of real and novel time in *Ulysses*, Joyce has been placed on the cutting edge, on the distinction between modernity and postmodernity. He has shown how time can be exposed as a limited conceptual and conventional apparatus, as an axis upon which historical events have been "meaningfully" plotted in succession or progression, and simultaneously, this conception of time is problematized as a universal standard. Similarly in physics, the Einsteinian relativity theory establishes how time is dependent upon velocity with regard to light-speed. When particle velocity equals light speed, our conception of time is infinite: it reaches its conceptual limit. *Light* and *Reason/ Words* have been connected through the biblical narrative, which implies that the parallel implosion of time in physics and literature is certainly not accidental.

Hegel has furnished *Reason* (*Light*) to be central to the purpose of History. His conception of *Reason/ Light* reaches the notion of *Absolute* through its articulation in National spirit that weaves together modern records. What constitutes the privileged position of the *Absolute*: Spirit, with regard to the *Universal: Reason*, and the *Particular: Nation*, is its self-reflective moment that is essential in the constitution God as *Absolute*. The *Absolute* (God) is primarily an object that also contains the subjective moment, and thus determines itself as the (only) exemplary *Universal*. The individual (Man, Universal) is both the subject and object of History: the subjective character (as in the oral account or storytelling) being always mastered/ negated. This reflective moment (of the universal as it is subjected to itself = *Absolute*) has found its hyperbolic use among modernist writers such as Joyce, portraying a picture within a picture, within a picture.... Hence, time as a linear sequence has no meaning because it has been caught within the loop of reflexivity. The Einsteinian limitation of time, i.e., time is infinite when particle velocity reaches the speed of light, when light reflects upon itself, is contemporary to Joyce's novel. The relation of *Light* and *Reason* is clear in religious representations of the words/ designs of God, as *Absolute*, and it demonstrates that we have reached the conceptual limits of our language, code, mode of representation as established by biblical narratives. Language is currently re-invented through the advent of simulation as third order simulacra. The progression of time as understood through the relation of past-present-future is dependent upon the construction of the event as historical, linear, Newtonian, and it is also under reconstruction.

Hyper-reflexivity of modernity has lead to postmodernity. A postmodern re-conceptualization of time has put to question historical succession as it has materialized in the proposed maneuvers to end History or conversely to end Philosophy. These discourses tend to construct philosophy in opposition to history, philosophy being the conception of a consciousness in the present time [subjective via objective], and history being its making through time [objective via subjective]. The unity of the two modes has been a Cartesian illusion: The "I" that thinks is judged to be the same as the "I" that has experienced "it." Kant has critiqued this move by proving that there cannot be an "I" [subject] without a "it" [object] (Kant, 1989). The "I" has been later secured by Hegel in that the "I" is not only defined only in its relation to an "it"[object]. Rather, for Hegel, the constitution of an "I," [subject] needs to be mirrored through a recognition of an-Other "I" [subject], through an understanding of a "We," [collectively]. (Hegel, 1971)

Both Kant and Hegel seem to be caught up in the opposition of subject/ object as constructed through active syntax. To lapse into passive verb constructions is one way of avoiding the impasse of the primary opposition between subjects and objects: cause and effect, in the construction of the event, and to obscure either the subject or the object depending on the particular stance one has on the issue of primacy, i.e., which term in the opposition came first. However, such stylistic devices [even though I have employed them plentifully] avoid addressing the key issue: the problematic construction of the opposition between subjects and objects that Kant articulated and Hegel tried to rescue through an additive synthesis of perspective, a "We" that is the *Absolute*: "I," particular; "it," universal. Hegel, thus, would see the historical process as the conception a "We," in particular the national spirit. History, as conceived by Hegel, is ultimately tied with the fate of the nation-state.[14]

Philosophy, however, is not necessarily opposed to history. To delineate a *historicophilosophical* approach has been a conceptual problem that many have tackled more or less successfully. Both philosophy and history negotiate the status of the event in the present and through time. However, the construction of events is not distinct from the construction of time; they are co-determined. The denaturing of time (to live without history or a leaving memory) is a postmodern effect (Hayles, 1990), but it does not mark the disappearance of history, rather its hyper-proliferation in media where time has become instantaneous, space irrelevant, and the event, as meaningful information/ news, has taken center stage. News, without the luxury of reflection, but rather in the outpouring of reports that are simulated through space to grant immediacy, that take the form of a briefing: condensed information stringed together. It no longer matters who does what to whom, but rather that something is occurring and that it is reported live for public spectacle, whether it is imaginary, real, or a mere projection. Before I move to see how the denaturing of time and its separation from space has affected medicine, let me take a close look at what Hegel tried to constitute as Philosophical History to see how his idealist construction of the

---

[14] "A community which acquires a stable existence and elevates itself into a state requires more than merely subjective mandates of government, sufficient only for the needs of the moment. It requires rules, laws, universal and valid norms [philosophy]. It thus produces a record of, and interest in, intelligent, definite, and in their effects lasting actions and events. To these, Mnemosyne [remembrance literally, history], in order to perpetuate the formation and constitution of the State, is impelled to add duration by remembrance." (Hegel, 1953: 76)

event has proliferated, and how it is later approached by Foucault through the genealogical, archeological, and strategic method, (Foucault, 1991) to see how his historicophilosophical approach has been derived primarily in resisting Hegel's absolutism.

Hegel has set out the relations of Logic [idea/ dialectic], Geometry [nature/ space], and History [spirit/time] in terms of thesis, antithesis, synthesis, where history is the very calumniation of philosophical *Reason* that grants meaning to events. Hegel, in *Reason In History*, sets out to establish how philosophy is always already embedded in history since "the sole thought which philosophy brings to the treatment of history is the simple concept of *Reason*: that *Reason* is the law of the world and that, therefore, in world history things come about rationally." (Hegel, 1953: 11) Foucault tries to exploit the space between *Reason* and unthought to show that in history all does not come in reason and providence, but rather that reason (in the form of expert opinion) is imposed upon history through power, and that it is a historical construction as well. He attempted to diagram the realm of the unthought, of folly (in *Madness and Civilization*) to demonstrate how history is not necessarily of/ in reason, and to work with reason so that strategies against the exertion of reason can be charted, knowing full well that his discourses may be used in the service of reason and not resistance. Foucault designs strategies that work vis-a-vis the globalizing moves of Hegel. But is Hegel totalizing in his use of reason as the foundation of history?

In Hegel, the circuit of power/ knowledge is closed through the spirit: "The principles of the national spirits progressing through a necessary succession of stages are only moments of one universal Spirit which through them elevates and completes itself into a self-comprehending totality." (Hegel, 1953: 95) It is clear: singularity in the manifestation of a comprehensive *Reason*, and it is to be regarded as the aim of national history. The spirit is both subjective and objective, therefore *Absolute* in its manifestation of *Reason*: a mere projection of rational subjects that need to suspend their disbelief in order to find *Reason*, to discover the Spirit? "That this Idea or reason is the True, the Eternal, the *Absolute* Power and that it and nothing but it, its glory and majesty, manifests itself in the world -- this, as we said before, has been proven in Philosophy and is being presupposed here as proved." (Hegel, 1953: 11) Is the employment of reason a self evident necessity in the making of the nationalist spirit that is a manifestation of the Spirit as *Absolute*?

I will briefly clarify what Hegel means by the Relation of *Absolute, Universal, Particular* and how his equation is rigged. First, I need to establish the Kantian differentiation between **bounds** and **limits**. Kant[15] draws the distinction between bound and limit mainly in the *Critique of Pure Reason*. Bounds are seen as mere negations or shadows that define objective presence, and limits

---

[15] "Limits (with extended being) always presuppose a space which is met with outside, a certain determinate place that encloses it; confines [schranken] require nothing of that sort, but are mere negations which affect a quantity insofar as it does not have absolute completeness." (Kant, 1953: § 57, IV, 352) Confines are synonyms for bounds that have been used here.

presuppose a positivity, an outside, and indicate another space where the object as defined by the bound may lose its present consistency. This distinction has been taken up by Hegel as well. Only for Hegel,[16] the limit becomes a reflection of the bound (boundary) onto itself and is unattainable: it is what the object (as conceived in language?) ought to be, yet what it always fails to be. The *a priori* failure of the object to reach its limit and thus move from the domain of the **Particular** to the **Universal** is where Hegel[17] locates the **Absolute** (both objective knowledge and knowing subject). The Universal is determined as an exceptional Particular (Hegel's justification of the Monarch's will as an embodiment of the state[18] develops this line of thought); however, his argument can be totalizing if a predetermined (by lineage, class, gender, race and so on) *Particular* is always established as the *Universal* through an arbitrary method of derivation, which conceals the lack or negative relationship of the *Universal* to itself, and to others.

Hegel attempts to curtail the object of Philosophy/ the subject of History before it reaches its limit by letting the limit be occupied by an exemplary, *Absolute* object (that is such because it embodies or contains subjectivity), and thus he secures the singularity of the Universal as the only possible object that is what it ought to be (the Monarch's words are always the Law: *Absolute*). The relation of the *Universal* to the *Particular* is that of exclusion or negation, whereas the *Absolute* pretends to contain in its interior the experience of all the particulars while it retains the form of the universal. The *Absolute*, thus, is a pure presence that negates the negation of the Universal. A rigged equation: since a double subtraction does not necessarily lead to an elevated whole. The totalizing moves of Hegel are founded upon the construction of a singular negative terrain as shaped by the exclusion of the universal, a singular fissure/ split, which can be regarded as the only *Absolute* as reflected upon itself. Objects, however, do reach their limits when the conceptual system by which they are determined becomes outmoded, when the distinction of figure and ground that has supported them is not definite, when the King's (Universal) arbitrariness is exposed, when "man would be erased, like a face drawn in the sand at the edge of the sea." (Foucault, 1973: 387)

For Foucault, the historicophilosophical practice "does not exclude any other" (Foucault, 1991: 391) any *Particular* in the privileging *Reason* or the *Universal*. Rather, this practice "is a matter of making one's own history, of fabricating as through fiction the history that would be traversed by the question of the relations between structures of rationality that articulate true discourse and

---

[16] "In being-there the determinacy is limit, restriction [bound]. Thus, otherness is not something-indifferent or outside it, but its own moment. In virtue of its quality, something is first finite and secondly alterable, so that finitude and alterability belong to its being." (Hegel, 1991: 148)

[17] "Certainly God is the object indeed *he is the object pure and simple*, as against which our particular (subjective) opinions and notions have neither truth nor validity. But precisely as absolute object, God does not confront subjectivity as a dark and hostile power; instead he contains it within himself as an essential moment." (Hegel, 1991: 272)

[18] This argument is made in Hegel's *Phenomenology of the Spirit*. I have accessed Jean Hyppolite translation. *La Phenomenology De L' Espirit*.

the mechanisms of subjugation that are tied to it." (Foucault, 1991: 391) To opt out of Hegelian blackmail, Foucault has examined ways to unravel the connection with and interest in a rational subject for the constitution of objective seeming, valid, true narratives that secure claims to power. To end history, because linearity, the national spirit, or universality, which have constituted it, are considered problematic, or to end philosophy, because history has overtaken it [birth of History of Consciousness], would be misleading. Both history and philosophy need to be re-thought to account for present contingent circumstances/ particulars. Foucault's local critique does establish a mode through which both subjectivity and objectivity are re-conceived not in their universal (other-negating) mode, but as partial.

Time is no longer an arrow pointing towards an unjustified, justifiable, or hostile telos as in eschatology. It is presented for what it always has been: a literary device that has shaped and structured the world when it was elevated to the status of universal through the circularity of the Spirit/ the phoenix myth. Time as sequence has implied that movement is always directed away from what is towards what might become. Such construction is based upon the conception of a human subject/ object of time and history. With the end of the human as proper subject (i.e., the birth of cyborgs), we can no longer arrive at consistent/ total ontology (through a subject/ object self-negating pair) or a singular directing vector. As such, time can no longer be viewed through linearity, but through a ceaseless movement that may no longer be directed by a will to power or a power/ knowledge. The telos that has directed the arrow of time has always been presupposed in the arche, the principle, the a priori, the universal as *Absolute*: God.

I have established how the universal, fixed by a priori grounds to the *Absolute*, is always ideologically invested; consequently, history as national origin finding is simply a legitimization story that justifies action, coercion, suppression. History conceived in this manner affects other modalities of history that are not of the national variety, i.e., even medical history, for example: the justification of containment for diseased individuals whatever scale or duration; the containment of mentally ill in asylums or other places of enclosure (even if they have been separate from criminals in Britain. The unthought as initially conceived by Foucault is not a singular, lumping domain); the medicalization of criminality that we have seen in the past few years (i.e., there is such a thing as a mass murderer personality), and so on. In fact the post-modern condition is about Modernity (Man/ Humanity/ Enlightenment) reaching its limit where what may follow is exposed to a radically critical mode of analysis that tests its validity as in the Kantian situation. Critique or in our age multivalent hypercritiques are the markers of conceptual unrest that wrestles to redefine the current state through new contesting and contested circumstances (particulars/ contingencies).

These questions can be posed: what bounds are presently negotiated and what will their projected limits be at least in the domain of knowledge that I have situated myself (primarily medicine)? Can a universal ground be a valid basis for decision making and if yes what would it be? Could we speak of progress, enlightenment as distinct from scientific triumphalism? Does a consensus always need to be reached or could we define productive movement through an evaluation of differences that does not however stabilize a singular figure/ ground contrast? I will describe how a partial determination of subject/ object avoids Hegel's totalizing, how partiality can be the basis for a more symbiotic model of governmentality that would have critique as its operative mode.

As such, "critique is the moment through which the subject gives itself the right to question truth concerning its power effects and to question power about its discourses of truth. Critique will be the art of voluntary inservitude, of reflective indocility. The essential function of critique would be that of desubjectification in the game of what one would call, in a word, the politics of truth." (Foucault, 1991: 386) Critique as a means of de-subjecting the speaker is also central to postmodern CyberFeminist considerations that determine how the body has always been the site of subjugation/ subjection through its making into the object/ subject of knowledge. Partial, unstable boarders between subject and object, make for provisional knowledges and records, and can be descriptive of the discursive chatter present in cyber-space, where one discovers a hyper-proliferation of simulated codes whether they are human/ animal/ machine.

3. Postmodern Considerations Or What Are Cyber Feminisms?

> Enlightenment is man's emergence from his self-incurred immaturity. Immaturity is the inability to use one's own understanding without the guidance of another. This immaturity is self-incurred if its cause is not lack of understanding, but rather lack of resolution and courage to use without the guidance of another. The motto of enlightenment is therefore Sapere aude! Have the courage to use your own understanding. (Kant, 1991: 58)

To represent enlightenment as the emergence from a self-incurred immaturity is problematic in that it presumes immaturity (which I take to mean something akin to false-consciousness) to be the result of one's own agency, so that all one would have to do is find in oneself the courage to think and critique, "to use one's own understanding." Critique, thus, is already presupposed as the only possible answer to ideology (false consciousness) as generated through an eager to please the status quo historicity. Immaturity is always ideological, in the service of power, and the call to use one's own ability to understand is to move into the realm of critique and voluntary inservitude. To use one's critical ability does not necessarily result in a singular version of enlightenment in the progressive variety, nor of an obscurity in the regressive variety. All that critique can offer (whether within reason or not) is to destabilize notions of

Absolute, of totality, of wholeness that effaces diversity. The question remains: what sort of agent can be constructed on the basis of resistance alone and how effective would such agency be?

Agency, another problematic concept, for Kant, would be emancipatory if it acquired the responsibility to think for one-self only on public affairs and under the label of the citizen. Citizen: land-owning, educated/ literate, aristocratic, males maybe a bit broader to include some from the rising mercantile class. The Kantian form of critique privileges writing/ publication, which could be anonymous although if necessary the person would be called to stand by what has been said if it is slanderous. Agency for Kant is not just to think (Descartes' famous "I think therefore I am"), but to write/ speak probably anonymously in order to critique common affairs in the public sphere with a regard towards common good, i.e., critique should always be tempered. Kant mentions in passing the "immaturity" of the "fairer" sex or "children," which for his time to even contemplate would have been regarded as revolutionary.

However, Kant's notion of agency cannot go far enough to "liberate" them as well since their "dependence" is essential in the constitution of singular Man (Lacan has thus utilized the social determination of this "dependence" to prove via Hegel that there is no such this as *The Woman*[19]). Foucault has challenged Kant's notion of emancipation as established upon the right to produce discourse since Foucault regarded the making of discourse as a subordination to reason, and thus to result in subjugation. (Discourses on sexuality have been established upon the confession ritual that presuppose sex to be sin.)[20] The act, for Foucault, can not be free speech (as it has been deemed in the constitution of the nation-state that is no longer a monarchy), rather the act is to transgress one's limitations, so that it would create the space necessary to re-invent oneself through discourse and experience, to move through radical alterity elsewhere.

The opposition of speech and experience has been destabilized by many feminists, to show that indeed subjectivity cannot contain or be contained in the mapped out body (as in the Freudian motto "anatomy is destiny," which no longer applies since prosthetics make the impossible possible: a Pregnant man/ mother[21]). Rather bodily conceptions and experience are simulated/ re-invented in cybernetic languages. The mirror that Hegel unknowingly constituted as another subject is necessary to stabilize an *I* through a *We*, and is clearly the site of modern identifications of the national, religious, or universal variety. However, the mirror is also refigured in cyberspace through the computer, where the image is substituted by the code, and identity does

---

[19] Lacan in "God And the *Jouissance* Of ~~The~~ Woman. A Love Letter" (*Feminine Sexuality*).
[20] Look at Foucault's *History of Sexuality: An Introduction.*
[21] More details with regard to a pregnant man look in "Reproducing The Posthuman Body: Ectogenetic Fetus, Surrogate Mother, Pregnant Man" by Susan M. Squire.

not pass through sameness [the thread that holds the "We" together as in the *Absolute*] but diversity.

Collectivity, therefore, can only be regarded as an assemblage of many rather than a collection of the same. Singular "ontology [has been], thus, [established] not [only as] a foundation, but a normative injunction that operates insidiously by installing itself into the political discourse as its necessary ground" (Butler, 1990: 148) To root subjectivity in the distinct experience of being the same is problematic since subjectivity has no longer any distinct character as it is represented only by an *I* that moves as easily from one to another. Thus, the *I* of subjectivity even when it refers to a particular body or context can at the same time resist to be fixed in any one situation. The *I* can move easily from one to another, to weave discourse through iteration, but not necessarily of identity as through its mirroring in the *We*, but rather alterity.

The *I* is a fissure that has been created by power, so that the individual body can apologize for its conduct [as in *docile bodies*], and reinforce power as through the representations of the scaffold in Foucault's *Discipline And Punish*. Even if subjectivity is constructed in the interest of power and through the performance of an identity function, identity can never be tautological, coherent, stable, singular. Identity has always been the function through which ideology is inserted, the genealogy of power legitimated, and is the tip from the iceberg of alterity. Bodies and identities are not equivalent even if they are situated on opposite sides of the equation of power. In order to destabilize the link between them one would have to engage in local critique and contestation. Clearly "situated purposes are necessarily finite, rooted in partiality and subtle play of same and different, maintenance and dissolution." (Haraway, 1991) The key to the destabilization of power/ knowledge is to problematize the process of production/ reproduction, is to destabilize the identity function (without being reductive about the type or form that power takes so that govermentality always remains an open field).

Thus, "to enter into the repetitive practices of this terrain of signification is not a choice, for the 'I' that might enter is always already inside: there is no possibility of agency or reality outside of the discursive practices that give those terms the intelligibility that they have. The task is not whether to repeat, but how to repeat or, indeed, to repeat and, through radical proliferation of gender [or other normative categories], to displace [unsettle] the very gender norms that have established repetition itself" (Butler, 1990: 148) through identification of the same. An escape from the body into cybernetic hyper-codes is not really possible even if identity boarders are questioned, and a total escape or liberation from the code is illusory because only within the code can communication and interconnectedness occur even if the code is not just language.

Since an escape outside the code or discourse is not possible, then the only maneuver possible is to radically resist the mode of inscription into the same and to continually implode singularity, to unmask it as ideological, a move that wishes to demonstrate "truth" through its grasp of power. "What is called for instance is an examination of the operation of the 'grammar' of each figure of discourse, its syntactic laws or requirements, its imaginary configurations, its metaphoric networks, and also, of course, what it does not articulate at the level of utterance: its silences," (Irigaray, 1985: 75) in order to find ways to articulate the unthought not in the interest of one but many. The importance of "'theory' lies in enactment and in writing strategies" (Kondo, 1990: 304), not just in the delineation of concepts. The status of fugitive is not a refusal to face some threat, but rather it is the desire to relocate in order to keep the prospect of freedom in the game of governing, to allow for openness, and to discover new spaces through transgression.

Subjectivity does not need the refuge of the *Absolute*. Its motion uncovers the space where it can operate not in the dialectical monopoly of reason, but in a dance of limit and transgression. Subjectivity should not be stabilized by a negating relation to the Other, nor with a self-negated relation to itself via a *We*. Subjectivity is an *i/t* that does not presume wholeness is ideal. Rather, *i/t* already sees itself backwards in a *t/i*, in the beginning of a quest/ion that has no end and no beginning. History is this account of splitting and reversing, where only questions can be posed and answers never stabilized. Philosophy and history are no longer opposed. They are the vehicles of subjectivity towards elsewhere: the goal may never be fixed. This age is about transgressing limits of identity and difference to reconstitute them, about breaking the Law of sameness to figure moves that preserve diversity, so that "nature and culture are reworked; the one can no longer be the resource for appropriation or incorporation by the other." (Haraway, 1991)

~.~.~

This is an age where transgression is simply breaking into a secure system, where knowledge can no longer be established upon a singular power base, where individuals and communities may still be trapped in the game of co-determination in the interest of governments and institutions. Even if we can have a glimpse of the broader level of sociality that is independent of these terms, the stories of co-determination are always about the materialization of our worst fears: disembodiment, catastrophes, fatalities, diseases, about marginalization in the name of these fears. What if we have not been able to keep up to the pace of the "fishes" that can transgress their pre-configured limitations, and we are left in the technological dust of the future before the game ever starts.

Can we change the script and imagine a more likable or fancied conclusion? a happy end? Cyber-Disney I am sure will make fortunes selling it to the hopefuls still frozen in nitrogen, anticipating.... Or conversely, we really learn how to live with each other and our prosthetics checks will revise our thoughts/ visions to make sure that we do not fixate on the same, that we will respect diversities, the planet, the universe, that we will become less self-centered. Then the term other-centered would acquire a meaning other than co-dependence or self-erasure.

Politics is really just that: the art of the possible projections whether it concerns medicine, education, or whatever. I believe I have illustrated enough of the ways in which it manipulates information and knowledge to display how the game can be changed, how power and knowledge do not need to collaborate behind our backs, how indeed we can all start dealing with the ways we are interested, and how we differ from others, to start negotiating on open terms the contours of the future. Otherwise, the negotiations will go on without us.

Works Cited

Abrams, Donald, I. (1985). "Issues Of The Medical Treatment of AIDS Relevant To Mental Health Practitioners." in *What To Do About AIDS: Physicians And Mental Health Practitioners Discuss The Issues.*

Aggleton, P., G. Hart, P Davies, eds. (1989). *AIDS, Social Representations, Social Practice.* London: Falmer.

Almond, Brenda. ed. (1990). *AIDS A Moral Issues: The Ethical, Legal And Social Aspects.* Mackmillans Press LTD: Houndmills, Basingstoke, Hampshire, and London.

Anderson, Warwick. (1993). "The New York Needle Trial: The Politics Of Public Health In The Age Of AIDS." in *AIDS and Contemporary History.*

Balsamo, Anne. (1996). *Technologies Of The Gendered Body: Reading Cyborg Women.* Duke University Press, Durham And London.

Barnes, David S. (1995). *The Making Of A Social Disease: Tuberculosis In Nineteenth-Century France.* University Of California Press: Berkeley, Los Angeles, London.

Barrett, Tom and Steve Pruitt. (1994). "Corporate Virtual Workspace" in *Cyberspace: First Steps.*

Baudrilard, Jean. (1994). *The Illusion Of The End.* trans. Chris Turner. Polity Press, Cambridge.

Benedikt, Michael. ed. (1994). *Cyberspace: First Steps.* MIT Press: Cambridge Massachusetts and London.

Berridge, Virginia, Philip Strong. eds (1993). *AIDS And Contemporary History.* Cambridge University Press.

Blank, Robert H. (1988). "Ethics And Policy: Issues In Biomedical Technology." in   *Technology And Politics.*

Bogard, William. (1996). *The Simulation Of Surveillance: Hypercontrol In Telematic Societies.* Cambridge University Press: Cambridge.

Borell, Merriley. (1993). "Training The Senses, Training The Mind" in *Medicine and the Five   Senses.*

Boulanger, G. R. (1969). "Prologue: What Is Cybernetics" in *Survey Of Cybernetics: A Tribute   To DR. Nobert Wiener.*

Brieger, Gert. (1993). "Sense And Sensibility In Late Nineteenth-Century Surgery In America" in *Medicine and the Five Senses.*

Butler, Judith. (1994). *Bodies That Matter: On The Discursive Limits of 'Sex.'* Routledge: New   York, London.

_____. (1990). *Gender Trouble: Feminism And The Subversion Of Identity.* Routledge: New   York, London.

Bynum, W. F. (1994). *Science And The Practice Of Medicine In The Nineteenth Century*. Cambridge University Press: Cambridge.

Casper, Monica J. (1995). "Fetal Cyborgs And Technomoms On The Reproductive Frontier: Which Way To Carnival?" in *The Cyborg Handbook*.

Clark, J. H. (1969). "Medical Cybernetics" in *Survey Of Cybernetics: A Tribute To DR. Nobert Wiener*

Clarke, Adele. (1996). "'Modernity, Postmodernity, & Reproductive Processes, ca. 1890-1990, or 'Mommy Where Do Cyborgs Come From Anyway?'" in *The Cyborg Handbook*

Clynes, Manfred, E. (1995). "Cyborg II: Sentic Space Travel." in *The Cyborg Handbook*.

Clynes, Manfred, E. and Nathan S. Kline. (1995). "Cyborgs In Space" in *The Cyborg Handbook*. Reprinted from *Astronautics*, September, 1960.

Crigger, Bette-Jane. ed. (1993). *Cases In Bioethics: Selections From The Hastings Center Report*. St. Martin's Press: New York.

Cunningham, Adrew. (1992). "Transforming the Plague: the laboratory and the identity of infectious disease" in *Laboratory Revolution In Medicine*.

Cunningham, Adrew and Perry Willans. eds. (1992). *Laboratory Revolution In Medicine*. Cambridge University Press.

DASPA. (1995). " Pilot's Associate" in *The Cyborg Handbook*.

Davis, Angela Y. (1983). *Women, Race, And Class*. Vintage Books: New York.

Demczynski, S. (1969). "The Tools Of The Cybernetic Revolution." in *Survey Of Cybernetics: A Tribute To DR. Nobert Wiener*

Derrida, Jacques. (1978a). "Structure Sign, and Play In The Discourse Of The Human Sciences." in *Writing And Difference*. The University Of Chicago Press: Chicago.

Dickson, David. (1993). "Towards A Democratic Strategy For Science: The New Politics Of Science" in *The 'Racial' Economy Of Science:: Toward A Democratic Future*.

Donne, John. (1624). *Devotions*. reprinted in John Donne. *Devotions upon Emergent Occasions*. Anthony Raspa. ed. Montreal and London: McGill-Queen's UP, 1975.

Einstein, Albert. (1993). *Relativity: The Special And General Theory*. Routledge: New York, London.

Featherstone, Mike and Roger Burrows. eds. (1995). *Cyberspace/ Cyberbodies/ Cyberpunk Cultures Of Technological Embodiment*. Sage Publications: London, Thousand Oaks, New Delhi.

Foucault, Michael. (1996). "What is Critique" in *What Is Enlightenment: Eighteenth-Century Answers And Twentieth Century Questions*.

_____. (1995). "Two Lectures" in *Critique and Power: Recasting The Foucault/ Habermas Debate*.

_____. (1994). *The Birth Of The Clinic: An Archeology Of Medical Perception*. Vintage Books Edition April 1994: New York.

_____. (1990). *The History Of Sexuality: An Introduction.* vol. 1. Vintage Books: New York.

_____. (1988). *The Care Of The Self: The History Of Sexuality Volume 3.* Vintage Books: New York, November.

_____. (1988). *Madness And Civilization: A History Of Insanity In The Age Of Reason.* trans. Richard Howard. Vintage Books: New York.

_____. (1979). *Discipline And Punish: The Birth Of The Prison.* Vintage Books: New York, February.

_____. (1973). *The Order Of Things: An Archaeology Of The Human Sciences.* Vintage Books: New York.

Fuchs, Cynthia J. (1995). "'Death I s Irrelevant' Cyborgs, Reproduction, And The Future Of Male Hysteria" in *The Cyborg Handbook.*

George, F. H. (1969). "Behavioural Cybernetics (Models Of Cognitive Behaviour)" in *Survey Of Cybernetics: A Tribute To DR. Nobert Wiener*

Gilbert, Nigel and Rosaria Conte. eds. (1995). *Artificial Societies: The Computer Simulation Of Social Life.* University Of College London Press: London.

_____. (1995). "Introduction: Computer Simulation For Social Theory" in *Artificial Societies: The Computer Simulation Of Social Life.*

Gilman, Sander. (1993). "Touch Sexuality and Disease" in *Medicine and the Five Senses.*

Goux, Jean-Joseph. (1990). *Symbolic Economies: After Marx And Freud.* trans by Jennifer Curtiss Cage. Cornell University Press: Ithaca, New York.

Gray, Chris Hables. ed. (1995). *The Cyborg Handbook.* Routledge: London and New York.

Gray, Chris Hables, Steven Mentor. (1995). "The Cyborgic Body Politic: Version 1.2." in *The Cyborg Handbook.*

Gray, Chris Hables, Steven Mentor, and Heidi J. Figueroa-Sarriera. (1995). "Cyborology: Constructing the Knowledge Of Cybernetic Organisms." in *The Cyborg Handbook.*

Grosz, Elizabeth. (1994). *Volatile Bodies: Toward A Corporeal Feminism.* Indiana University Press: Bloomington, Indianapolis.

_____. (1989). *Sexual Subversion: Three French Feminists.* Allen & Unwin Pty Ltd: Australia.

Habermas, Jurgen. (1995). "Some Questions Concerning The Theory Of Power: Foucault Again" in *Critique and Power: Recasting The Foucault/ Habermas Debate*

Haraway, Donna, J. (1995). "Cyborgs And Symbionts: Living Together In The New World Order" in *The Cyborg Handbook.*

_____. (1993a). "Cyborgs At Large: Interview With Donna Haraway." Interviewers: Constance Penley and Andrew Ross in *Technoculture.*

_____. (1993b). "The Actors Are Cyborgs, Nature Is Coyote, And The Geography Is Elsewhere: Postscript To 'Cyborgs At Large'" in *Technoculture.*

_____. (1991). *Simians, Cyborgs, And Women: The Reinvention Of Nature*. Routledge: New   York.

_____. (1989a). "The Biopolitics Of Postmodern Bodies: Determinations Of Self In Immune System Discourse." *Differences*, Winter 1989. vol. 1. no 1.

_____. (1989b). *Primate Visions: Gender, Race, and Nature in the World Of Modern Science*. Routledge: New York, London.

Harding, Sandra. ed. (1993). *The 'Racial' Economy Of Science: Toward A Democratic Future*. Indiana University Press, Bloomington And Indianapolis.

_____. (1993). "Introduction: Eurocentric Scientific Illiteracy -- A Challenge For The World Community" in *The 'Racial' Economy Of Science: Toward A Democratic Future*.

Hartouni, Valerie. (1991). "Containing Women: Reproductive Discourse In The 1980s." in *Technoculture*.

Hayles, Katherine. (1991). *Chaos Bound: Orderly Disorder In Contemporary Literature And Science*. Cornell University Press: Ithaca, London.

Hegel, G. W. F. (1991). *The Encyclopaedia Logic: Part I Of The Encyclopaedia Of Philosophical Sciences with the Zusätze*. trans. T. F. Geraets, W.A. Suchting, H.S. Harris. Hackett Publishing Co., Inc.: Indianapolis, Cambridge.

_____. (1985). *Hegel's Introduction To The Lectures On The History Of Philosophy*. trans. T. M. Knox and A. V. Miller. Clarendon Press: Oxford.

_____. (1971). *Le Phenomenology De L' Espirit*. tome II. trans. Jean Hyppolite. Aubier, Éditions Montaigne: Paris.

_____. (1953). *Reason In History: A General Introduction To The Philosophy Of History*. Macmillan Publishing Co.: New York, or Collier Macmillan Publishers: London.

Hirsch, Marianne and Evelyn Fox Keller. eds. (1990). *Conflicts In Feminism*. Routledge: New York, London.

Hobbes, Thomas. (1965). *Leviathan Or The Matter, Forme, & Power Of A Common-Wealth Ecclesiastical and Civil*. orig. pub. 1651. Penguin: London.

Hogle, Linda, F. (1995). "Tales From The Cryptic: Technology Meets Organism in The Living Cadaver." in *Cyborg Handbook*.

Irigaray, Luce. (1985). *This Sex Which Is Not One*. Cornell University Press: Ithaca, New York.

Journal Of Medicine And Philosophy, The. (Nov. 1987). *Michel Foucault And The Philosophy Of Medicine*. **vol.** 12, **no** 4.

Joyce, James. (1993). *Ulysses*. Oxford University Press: Oxford.

Kant, Immanuel. (1996). "What is Enlightenment?" in *What Is Enlightenment Eighteenth-Century Answers And Twentieth-Century Questions*.

_____. (1989). *Critique Of Pure Reason*. trans. Wolfgang Schwarz. Scientia Verlag Aalen: Germany.

_____. (1970). *Kant: Political Writings.* ed. Hans Reiss. trans. H. B. Nisbet. Cambridge University Press: Cambridge.

_____. (1970a). "Conjectures On The Beginning Of Human History" in *Kant: Political Writings.*

_____. (1953). *Prolegomena To Any Future Metaphysics That Will Be Able To Present Itself As A Science.* Manchester University Press: Manchester.

Kelly, Michael. ed. (1995). *Critique And Power: Recasting The Foucault/ Habermas Debate.* MIT Press: Cambridge, Massachusetts and London.

Kellogg, Wendy, A., John M. Carroll, and John T. Richards.(1994). "Making Reality A Cyberspace." in *Cyberspace First Steps.*

Kemp, Martin. (1993). "'The Mark Of Truth': Looking And Learning In Some Anatomical Illustration From Renaissance And The Eighteenth Century." in *Medicine and the Five Senses.*

Kondo, Dorinne K. (1990). *Crafting Selves: Power, Gender, And Discourses Of Identity In A Japanese Workplace.* University of Chicago Press: Chicago, London.

Kraft, Michael E., Norman J. Vig. eds. (1988). *Technology And Politics.* Duke University Press, Durham And London.

Lacan, Jacques. (1991). *The Seminar Of Jacques Lacan: Book I Freud's Papers on Technique 1953-1954.* trans. John Forrester. W. W. Norton & Company: New York, London.

_____. (1985). *Feminine Sexuality: Jacques Lacan And The Ecole Freudienne.* eds. Juliet Mitchell and Jacqueline Rose. trans, Jacqueline Rose. W. W. Norton CO: New York, London.

_____. (1981). *The Four Fundamental Concepts of Psycho-Analysis.* W. W. Norton & Company: New York, London.

_____. (1977). *Ecris: A Selection..* W. W. Norton & Company: New York, London.

Lawrence, Christopher. ed. (1992). *Medical Theory, Surgical Practice: Studies In The History Of Surgery.* Routledge: London And New York.

Lazreg, Marnia. (1990). "Feminism And Difference: The Perils Of Writing As A Woman On Women In Algeria" in *Conflicts In Feminism.*

Lewis, Jane. (1993). "Public Health: Doctors And AIDS As A Public Health Issue" in *AIDS And Contemporary History.*

Logan, Peter, M. (1991). "Conceiving The Body: Realism And Medicine In Middlemarch." *History Of The Human Sciences.* June, vol. 4. no 2.

Lyotard, Jean-Francois. (1991). *The Postmodern Condition: A Report On Knowledge.* trans. Geoff Bennington and Brian Massumi. University Of Minnesota Press: Minneapolis.

Mann, Jonathan, Dianiel J. M. Tarantola, Thomas W. Netter. eds. (1992). *A Global Report: AIDS In The World.* Harvard University Press: Cambridge, Massachusetts and   London, England.

Marx, Karl and Frederick Engels. (1991). *The German Ideology.* International Publishers: New York.

McKusick, Leon. ed. (1986). *What To Do About AIDS: Physicians And Mental Health Practitioners Discuss The Issues.* University of California Press: Berkeley, Los Angeles, London.

Morin, Stephen. (1986). "AIDS: Public Policy And Mental Health Issues" in *What To Do About AIDS: Physicians And Mental Health Practitioners Discuss The Issues.*

Nietzsche, Friedrich. (1980). *On The Advantage And Disadvantage Of History For Life.* Hackett Publishing Company, Indianapolis, Cambridge.

--------------. (1956). *The Birth Of Tragedy And The Genealogy Of Morals.* trans. Francis Golffing. Anchor Books Doobleday: New York, London, Toronto, Sydney, Auckland.

Oehlert, Mark. (1995). "From Captain America To Wolverine: Cyborgs In Comic Books, Alternative Images Of Cybernetic Heroes And Villains." in *The Cyborg Handbook.*

Orr, Alistair. (1990). "The Legal Implications Of AIDS and HIV Infection In Britain And The United States." in *AIDS A Moral Issue: The Ethical, Legal And Social Aspects.*

Pask. G. (1969). "Learning And Teaching Systems" in *Survey Of Cybernetics: A Tribute To DR. Nobert Wiener*

Penley, Constance and Andrew Ross. eds. (1991). *Technoculture.* University of Minnesota Press: Minneapolis, Oxford.

Pollak, Michael, Genevieve Paicheler, Janine Pierret. (1992). *AIDS: A Problem For Sociological Research.* Sage: London.

Porter, Arthur. (1969). *Cybernetics Simplified.* The English Universities Press, LTD: London.

Porter, Roy. (1995). *Discovering The History Of Psychiatry.* Oxford University Press, Oxford.

_____. (1993). "The Rise of Physical Examination" in *Medicine And The Five Senses.*

_____. ed. (1992). *The Popularization of Medicine 1650-1850.* Routledge, London and New   York.

_____. (1992a*). Doctor Of Society: Thomas Beddoes And The Sick Trade In Late-Enlightenment England.* Routledge: London, New York.

_____. (1992b). "Spreading Medical Enlightenment: The Popularization Of Medicine In Georgian England, And Its Paradoxes." in *The Popularization of Medicine 1650-1850.*

Porter, Roy and W. F. Bynum. eds. (1993). *Medicine and the Five Senses.* Cambridge University Press.

Poster, Mark. (1991). "Postmodern Virtualities." in *Cyberspace/ Cyberbodies/ Cyberpunk: Cultures Of Technological Embodiment*

Proctor, Robert. (1993). "Nazi Medicine And The Values In Science." in *The 'Racial' EconomyOf Science: Toward A Democratic Future.*

Ramazanoglu, Caroline. ed. (1993). *Up Against Foucault: Explorations Of Some Tensions Between Foucault And Feminism.* Routledge: London, New York.

Reiser, Stanley J. (1993). "Technology And The Use Of The Senses In Twentieth-Century Medicine" in Medicine And The Five Senses.

Rescher, Nicholas. (1993). Pluralism: Against The Demand For Consensus. Clarendon Press: Oxford.

Rose, J. ed. (1969). Survey Of Cybernetics: A Tribute To DR. Nobert Wiener. Iliffe Books LTD: London.

Rosen, Michael. (1996). On Voluntary Servitude: False Consciousness And The Theory Of Ideology. Polity Press: Cambridge.

Rosie, A. M. (1969). "Cybernetics and Information (Information Theory Problems)" in A Survey   Of Cybernetics: A Tribute To DR. Nobert Wiener.

Ross, Andrew. (1991). "Hacking Away At The Counterculture." in Technoculture.

Rothman, Sheila M. (1994). Living In The Shadow Of Death: Tuberculosis And The Social Experience Of Illness In American History. Johns Hopkins University Press: Baltimore and London.

Rushing, William A. (1995). The AIDS Epidemic: Social Constructions Of An Infectious Disease. Westview Press: Boulder, San Francisco, Oxford.

Saussure, F. de. (1974). A Course In General Linguistics. Fontana/ Collins: New York.

Savitt, Todd, L. (1978). Medicine And Slavery: The Diseases And Health Care Of Blacks In Antebellum Virginia. University of Illinois Press: Urbana, Chicago, and London.

Sawday, Jonathan. (1995). The Body Emblazoned: Dissection And The Human Body In Renaissance Culture. Routledge: London and New York.

Schmidt, James. ed. (1996). What Is Enlightenment Eighteenth-Century Answers And Twentieth-Century Questions. University of California Press: Berkeley, Los Angeles, London.

Seltzer, Mark. (1992). Bodies And Machines. Routledge, New York And London.

Shields, Rod. ed. (1996). Cultures Of Internet: Virtual Spaces, Real Histories, Living Bodies. Sage Publications: London, Thousand Oaks, New Delhi.

Shilts, Randy. (1987). And The Band Played On: Politics, People, And The AIDS Epidemic. Penguin Books: New York.

Squier, Susan M. (1996). "Reproducing The Posthuman Body: Ectogenetic Fetus, Surrogate Mother, Pregnant Man." in Posthuman Bodies.

Steele, Jack E. (1995). "How Did We Get There?" in The Cyborg Handbook.

Stepan, Nancy Leys and Sander L. Gilman. (1993). "Appropriating The Idioms Of Science: The Rejection Of Scientific Racism." in The 'Racial' Economy Of Science: Toward A   Democratic Future.

Stone, Allucquere Rosanne. (1994). "Will The Real Body Please Stand Up?: Boundary Stories   About Virtual Cultures." in Cyberspace: First Steps.

Third World Network. (1993). "Modern Science In Crisis: A Third World Response." in The 'Racial' Economy Of Science: Toward A Democratic Future.

Tomas, David. (1994). "Old Rituals For New Space: Rites de Passage And William Gibson's Cultural Model Of Cyberspace." in Cyberspace: First Steps.

Towers, Bridget. (1993). "Politics And Policy: Historical Perspectives On Screening" in AIDS Contemporary History.

Treichler, Paula A. (1991). "How To Have A Theory In An Epidemic: The Evolution Of AIDS Treatment And Activism" in Technoculture.

Virilo, Paul. (1994). The Vision Machine. trans. Julie Rose. Indiana University Press: Bloomington.

Wajcman, Judy. (1991). Feminism Confronts Technology. Pennsylvania State University Press, University Park, Pennsylvania.

Weeks, Jeffrey (1989). "AIDS: The Intellectual Agenda," in AIDS, Social Representations, Social Practice.

_____. (1993). "AIDS And The Regulation Of Sexuality" in AIDS And Contemporary History.

Woolley, Benjamin. (1994). Virtual Worlds: A journey in Hype and Hyperreality. Blackwell: Cambridge Mass., Oxford UK.

Zizek, Slavoj. (1994a). The Metastases Of Enjoyment: Six Essays On Women And Causality. Verso: London, New York.

_____. (1994b). Tarrying With The Negative: Kant, Hegel, And The Critique Of Ideology. Duke University Press, Durham.

_____. (1992). Enjoy Your Symptom: Jacques Lacan In Hollywood And Out. Routledge: New York, London.

_____. (1991). For They Know Not What They Do: Enjoyment As A Political Factor. Verso: London, New York.

_____. (1989). The Sublime Object Of Ideology. Verso: New York, London.